FOOD FOR
thought

A CULINARY TOUR OF
BRITAIN'S SEAS AND SKIES

SIMON COURTAULD

ILLUSTRATIONS BY LUCY VICKERY

THINK
BOOKS

A Think Book

First published in 2006 by
Think Publishing
The Pall Mall Deposit
124-128 Barlby Road, London W10 6BL
www.think-books.com

Distributed in the UK and Ireland by Macmillan Distribution Ltd.
Brunel Road, Houndmills, Basingstoke RG21 6XS

Distributed in the USA and Canada by Sterling Publishing Co., Inc.
387 Park Avenue South, New York, NY 10016-8810

Illustrations: Lucy Vickery
Editor: Emma Jones
Sub Editor: Rob Turner
Design: Lou Millward

ISBN-10: 1-84525-031-1
ISBN-13: 978-1-84525-031-7

Printed and bound in Singapore by Tien Wah Press
The publisher and author have made every effort to ensure the accuracy
and currency of the information in *Food for Thought*. We apologise for any
unintentional errors or omissions. The publisher and author disclaim any liability,
loss, injury or damage incurred as a consequence, directly or indirectly, of the use
and application of the contents of this book.
Cover image: Maximilian Weinzierl / Alamy

Preface

There is a well-known psalm which speaks of the fowls of the air and the fishes of the sea. Insofar as they make good eating, they are the subject of this book, which follows the same formula as the previous volume, *Food for Thought: A Culinary Tour of the English Garden*. The various species of fish and shellfish, worldwide, number more than 20,000; however, this book is confined to those fish which are found in European waters (not forgetting those that live in fresh water). I am, of course, conscious of the need for conservation of fish stocks and sustainable fishing, but I see no reason, for instance, to discourage the buying of cod. Its stocks in the North Sea may be dangerously low, but 95 per cent of the cod we eat is caught outside those fishing grounds.

The word 'fowl' no longer embraces all birds, but is restricted to domestic poultry and wild ducks and geese. While I have covered the principal feathered creatures which we eat these days, I have omitted small birds which are rarely available for sale and those which are no longer shot for the table.

As in the previous book, I have added practical tips at the foot of each piece, and listed a few suppliers at the end of the book. These essays first appeared in *The Spectator*, and my grateful thanks go to the former editor, Boris Johnson, and the present editor, Matthew d'Ancona, who published them, to the arts editor, Liz Anderson, who dealt with them so competently, and to Lucy Vickery who has illustrated them so beautifully.

Contents

Haddock

Haddock is fished from the north Atlantic, the Irish Sea, the seas around the Faroe Islands and Iceland, but I always associate it with the North Sea, and more particularly with the east coast of Scotland which has given us Finnan haddies and Arbroath smokies. The Finnan haddock takes its name from the village of Findon, which is south of Aberdeen in Scotland, where the fish used to be smoked over peat or seaweed. The Arbroath haddock differs from all others by being hot-smoked and not split open, giving the skin a coppery colour and the almost white flesh a most delicate flavour. (A surprising number of people believe an Arbroath smokie to be a herring; it would make a good question for the *Who Wants To Be A Millionaire?* game show.)

Haddock can be eaten fresh, but it is rarely found unfilleted at a fishmonger's. I wonder how many would know at once from Lucy Vickery's illustration (left) – its brownish-grey colour, with a black lateral line and John Dory-like 'thumbprint' – that this is a haddock. I know there are those who judge fresh haddock to be superior to cod, but I think that, in the world of white fish, a baked fresh codling is hard to beat. Haddock comes into its own when smoked; when the French speak of '*le haddock*' they are referring to the smoked fish, which they are inclined to offer as part of a *salade tiède*.

Haddock are brined before being hung up to dry and smoked, often over oak sawdust, until the flesh turns a pale straw colour. Why anyone should want to buy the bilious dyed haddock is beyond me. If the yellow is so attractive in certain dishes, or to certain cooks, it can be achieved, with flavour, by adding saffron, turmeric or mustard. The classic smoked haddock dishes – kedgeree, omelette Arnold Bennett, Cullen skink, haddock Monte Carlo – have no need of additional flavours. I know that recipes for kedgeree, from the Indian dish *khichri*, may contain a sprinkling of curry powder, but I prefer it without, also without onion or hard-boiled eggs. When eaten for breakfast it should, in my view, consist only of the flaked fish, rice, a little cream and chopped parsley or chives, with a poached egg on top.

Whoever first brought smoked haddock to the breakfast table deserves some sort of recognition. The dish known as haddock Monte Carlo was apparently invented for those tired and jaded after a night's gambling in the casino. The haddock is simmered in milk, which is then used to make a white sauce, with or without grated cheese, to be poured over the fish and poached eggs. Smoked haddock goes equally well with other breakfast foods – scrambled eggs, bacon, tomatoes – or the cooked fish may simply be mixed with cream, warmed in the oven and eaten on buttered toast with plenty of black pepper.

I was a bit nervous of making an omelette Arnold Bennett (the novelist was a great patron of the Savoy Grill, which created the dish for him), but it is really quite simple. Once the haddock has been simmered in milk and water, with bay leaf and onion slices, the omelette should be conventionally cooked but, while the eggs are still runny on top, add the flaked fish plus cream and grated Parmesan cheese, keep it all flat in the pan and finish under a hot grill. As a supper dish, I cannot recommend it too highly.

Connoisseurs of smoked haddock will tell you there is no substitute for Finnan haddock – the flesh is finer, the flavour subtler, etc, than any other haddock smoked elsewhere – but, in the south at least, you don't often find it so named. The Finnan haddie, they say, should be used, skin, bones and all, in the making of a classic Cullen skink. In the absence of the Finnan, simmer a smoked haddock fillet in milk and butter in which diced potatoes and onion have already been cooking, then discard any skin and bone and add cream and chopped parsley.

One could go on to talk about haddock flan, haddock soufflé, haddock mousse with horseradish sauce, haddock with Welsh rarebit, and other ways of treating this quintessentially British fish. The best news is that there is no shortage of haddock with which to indulge ourselves. While cod and other species are in dangerous decline, haddock stocks in the North Sea are now healthier than they have been for 30 years.

Although this fish is mainly eaten smoked, fresh haddock, especially the smaller ones, can rival fresh cod. And it is much more abundant around British coasts.

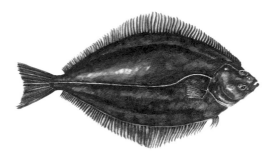

Halibut

There is plenty of life, as well as recent death, in a fish market. For its colour and noise and atmosphere, the market by the Rialto Bridge in Venice is as fascinating to me as a visit to the Scuola degli Schiavoni to see the Carpaccios. To buy, or just to admire, the fish landed on the Spanish Mediterranean coast I would highly recommend the Boqueria in Barcelona; and there is no better place than the wholesale market in Vigo to see the variety of Atlantic fish which are unloaded on to the quay throughout the night. Although I have never been to the famous market at Boulogne, a friend urged me to go to Lorient on the Brittany coast when I was staying nearby a few years ago. I remember cursing him because I lost my way in the town on a miserably wet morning before dawn, but I also recall the highlight of the market that day – a monster halibut, gaffed and strung up and looking like some sort of flying saucer.

The weight of this great flatfish was announced; it was, I think, about 200 pounds, although I have forgotten the exact figure. *The Cook's Encyclopaedia* by Tom Stobart claims that a halibut may be 15 feet long and weigh as much as 1,300 pounds, although Alan Davidson, in *North Atlantic Seafood*, refers to a maximum size of 600-700 pounds. In either case, such a fish would make a lot of steaks, and a lot of money at around £7 per pound.

That Lorient fish was unlikely to have ended up on French tables; indeed it was something of a surprise that a halibut should have been caught so far south. The species is found mainly in north British and Arctic waters, and for that reason is seldom used in French cooking. No mention is made of the *flétan* in Elizabeth David's books. When I inquired after halibut at the Newlyn fish market in Cornwall last year, I was told that one had been landed about five years ago. It is so little known in Spain that it is called only by its Latin name, *hippoglossus* (*hipogloso*). I have seen halibut in a Spanish cookbook translated as *rape*, but that is monkfish (no possible relation).

Forgetting the foreign names, the important thing when buying halibut is not to be fobbed off with Greenland halibut. This is a smaller and inferior fish, which has very little merit. If you can see the skin of the fish, the ersatz Greenland's underside is dark grey or brown, while that of the proper halibut is white. Real halibut, when sold as small, whole fish, are usually called chicken halibut.

Halibut is, in my view, one of the best white fish. Most books refer to its tendency to become dry when cooked, but this can be easily overcome, either by wrapping the fish steaks in buttered foil or by slow poaching. If cooked in foil, parsley, sorrel and a little wine could be added; if poached, Rick Stein recommends very gentle cooking in olive oil, with the addition of cucumber and dill. In her first cookbook Lady Maclean (who died in 2005) gives her Argyllshire recipe for frying halibut on the bone in butter and pouring over it a mixture of cream, Worcester sauce and lemon juice.

From the Hebrides, where halibut should be plentiful, I am tempted by a recipe from Rosemary Shrager, who used to run a cookery school on the Isle of Harris. Using halibut fillets, which are baked, she puts them on a bed of flageolet beans, previously soaked, which have been cooked in fish stock together with onion, garlic, tomatoes, carrots, parsley and coriander. Jennifer Paterson, when she used to entertain us in the 1980s at what one could almost call her weekly lunches at *The Spectator* (she was so much more than a cook), once did a halibut first course when the Prince of Wales was a guest. The fish, which had to be sent down from Scotland at a cost of something like £80, was cut into strips, which were then marinated overnight in fresh lime juice, with sliced onion and sea salt. They were offered to the honoured guest with the best olive oil and chopped parsley, but it is not recorded whether he appreciated this delicious extravagance.

Halibut is also well-known in northern Canada and Alaska, but I'm not sure it is properly appreciated there. Recipes involve cooking the fish variously with blue cheese, honey, and even – can you believe it? – plum sauce and 'a strawberry and jalapeno pepper salsa'. The best advice is always worth repeating: when you have a really good fish, don't bugger it about.

Greenland halibut is only worth eating when smoked; otherwise, go for the real fresh thing. Halibut liver-oil capsules, rich in vitamins A and D, are good for arthritis.

Pheasant

It is one of life's mysteries that, outside the circle of those involved in game shooting in Britain, so few pheasants are bought and eaten in a country where between 15 and 20 million birds are reared each year. I have wondered if the association of pheasants with wartime food – during the winter of 1940 the shooting season was extended into February to provide an additional stock of meat – may provide part of the answer. This may once have been so, but surely not now. The likely explanation has to do with a fear of the unfamiliar, and of breaking a tooth on a random pellet which may still be in the body of the pheasant, or possibly a distaste for birds that have been gunned down in a revolting blood sport (rather than strangled to death or electrocuted, as happens with chickens).

Most supermarkets, perhaps fearing expensive legal actions from customers with broken teeth, are reluctant to sell pheasants. So what is happening to the millions of birds shot every year? Some, of course, are eaten through the season and stored in the freezer; others are exported to France, Belgium and Germany, where there is a ready market. But the price obtainable for a brace in the feather is so ludicrously low that there have been dark rumours of large numbers of pheasants being buried at the end of a shooting day.

The Game Conservancy Trust and The British Association for Shooting and Conservation have been doing their best to promote game as low-fat, high-protein, healthy meat. How could anyone resist the offer from our local farm shop this month of three brace of pheasants, plucked and dressed, for £10, which is little more than £1.50 a bird? Properly cooked, and having been properly hung, a pheasant is one of the best eating birds, it has far more flavour and is often cheaper than chicken, and it is truly 'free-range'.

There are many who will say that the only way to eat a pheasant is to roast it, covered with strips of bacon, in a hot oven for 45 minutes. Gravy, bread sauce, fried breadcrumbs and chips are the usual accompaniments, plus a green vegetable – sprouts or cabbage – and a root such as Jerusalem artichoke. The only tips I can add are to use the more tender hen bird if possible and, since the flesh may be dry if overcooked, stuff the body with some bread soaked in sherry. I also like to eat game with cranberry sauce.

While not disputing for a moment that roast pheasant can be a wondrous thing, there are other options for cooking the several birds which may be in the freezer, especially the older cocks. Some of us may have had more than enough pheasant casseroles, made in the hope of masking the scrawny, badly shot birds which would be better made into sausages or croquettes. But the legs can be discarded while something delicious is done with the breasts.

Pheasant *Normande* is a dish which works well, combining sliced apples, cream and Calvados, with the breasts cooked in butter in a heavy pan. In a simpler version of this, the whole bird is browned in butter, then cooked in cream with white wine or a little lemon juice. Once this sauce has been reduced, it should be poured over the carved pheasant on a bed of peas and perhaps braised turnips. The gaminess of a well-hung bird can be successfully offset by a root vegetable, or by the bitterness of chicory. With cold pheasant my favourite thing, thanks to Delia Smith, is what she calls a cranberry and onion confit, made by stewing onions, garlic and sugar, then adding fresh cranberries, the zest and juice of an orange and some crushed cardamom seeds. Cook this gently for about an hour and allow it to get cold. It will last for weeks in the fridge.

Several books give a recipe for Circassian or Georgian pheasant, with a nod to that part of the world where Jason and his Argonauts supposedly discovered the bird, living on the banks of the River Phasis which separated Europe and Asia. I have not tried the dish, which uses walnuts, grapes, orange juice, Madeira and green tea, and am inclined to leave it to the natives of the Caucasus.

A better idea, which I pass on as the season comes to an end, has been put to me on two occasions while I was out shooting this month. Why not use these surplus, apparently unwanted pheasants to make pasties? A cousin of mine in Devon has already experimented, chopping up the meat with onion, garlic, bacon and herbs, and a man in Lincolnshire is marketing them in a small way. This is a business which should be expanded.

Not only is pheasant one of the best food bargains to be had, but it can also be frozen for months without coming to any harm. If you are offered a bird in the feather, check for indications of age – long spurs and horny feet.

Clams

If America can be associated with one shellfish more than any other, it must surely be the clam. I know that New England is supposedly the home of the clam bake, but you can't go far in any state without meeting clams in some form – raw in the shell, clam chowder, clam juice or that irresistible Clamato juice, of which there is far too little sold in this country. In Utah this month (for the skiing, not the Mormons), I had a delicious dish of steamed clams in a thin saffron sauce with coriander leaves, and on another occasion, after a glorious day in the mountains, a thick clam chowder with potato and bacon was served after three different sorts of oyster and before three varieties of crab – Alaskan King, Snow and Dungeness. Let no one say that you can't eat well in middle America.

It is not only the Americans who give their clams odd names (quahog, pismo, geoduck, littleneck). In Europe, we have the smooth venus, warty venus and carpet-shell. This last named, which is the one most commonly available, sounds much better in other languages: it is the *palourde* of France, the *vongola* of Italy and the *almeja* of Spain. *Palourdes farcies grillées*, well known in the kitchens and restaurants of Brittany, cannot be equalled, according to Jane Grigson, 'for piquancy and delight' (she applies her comment equally to oysters and mussels cooked in the same way). The clams, when opened, are covered with butter to which crushed garlic, chopped shallot and parsley have been added. They are then sprinkled with breadcrumbs and grated Gruyère cheese and baked in the oven. An outstanding little starter, as I have confirmed at home.

The recipe for *spaghetti alle vongole* involves a sauce made with olive oil, onion, garlic, tomatoes, parsley and some of the clam liquor. The Spanish dish of *almejas a la marinera* is made with the same sauce ingredients, minus the tomatoes, plus paprika and white wine. In England, cockles could be substituted, as long as they have not been steeped in vinegar. My impression is that we have fewer cockle beds these days, and I have noticed that cockles preserved in jars are often labelled 'Produce of Holland'.

Clams or cockles may be used to make fritters, chopped and beaten with egg yolks, breadcrumbs, herbs, milk and the stiffened egg whites to make a batter. They also make an acceptable savoury rolled in bacon, fried briefly and served on buttered toast as a poor man's Angel-on-Horseback. While on the subject, one might mention winkles (for which a pin is essential to extract them from their shells) and whelks, disappointing if overcooked, but delicious in France (*bulots*) with wine vinegar and chopped shallots. I have eaten another bivalve in the Channel Islands called *amande*, but found it to be chewy.

My current favourite, though, in the molluscan department is the razor-clam, which I first came across in northern Spain (*navaja*). They are now appearing on fishmongers' slabs in Britain and I am intrigued to know how they are gathered. They look a bit like those old razors which were sharpened with a strop, they bury themselves vertically in the sand and, in my experience, cannot easily be tempted to the surface. I was advised to go to a certain place, at a very low spring tide, on the north Cornish coast with a jar of cooking salt and look for the holes made by the razor-clams. A little salt poured into the hole would bring the creature to the surface when it could be grabbed, with a gloved hand to avoid cutting yourself on the sharp-edged shell.

I'm afraid I have to report that this clam hunt was a total failure. There were three of us armed with plenty of salt, but I think we may have driven our quarry deeper into the sand by smothering them with the salt. I was relieved to read that Alan Davidson had a similarly blank experience when he salted the razor-clam holes in the Orkneys (where these 'spoots', so called, are highly prized). On the west coast of America they use a 'clam gun', with a steel tube and suction, to draw up this buried treasure. This may be the preferred commercial method, but I would be glad to hear of any other ideas.

Once you have enough, they may be steamed briefly in a little wine and eaten with garlic and parsley like other clams, or cooked Chinese-style with black beans and chilli, as demonstrated by Rick Stein on one of his television programmes. Ginger, soy sauce and spring onions also go into the recipe, which I imagine would be equally good with crab or lobster.

Since writing the above, I have enjoyed some success in catching razor-clams. Having poured a little salt into the holes, it may be necessary to wait up to a minute for a low gurgling sound, which indicates that the razor-clam is about to surface. Sometimes they throw themselves out and on to the sand.

Monkfish

In the beginning was the angler-fish, so called because of the fishing rod or aerial on top of its head which, with a piece of tissue on the end serving as bait, waves above the sand in which the fish is lurking and attracts smaller fish to within devouring distance. It was a hideous fish which the cat would consent to eat if nothing better were offered, but it was not generally acknowledged as fit for human consumption. Angler-fish does not rate a mention from Mrs Beeton or Constance Spry, or from Elizabeth David in her books on Mediterranean and French cooking. Then – in which year or even which decade I cannot discover – the angler-fish disappeared and was reinvented as the monkfish. It is still the same fish, with the same ugly, flat head, wide mouth, fearsomely sharp teeth and Mick Jagger-like lips, although it seems to lose its fishing rod before appearing on a fishmonger's slab. But it is no longer considered to be cat food now; it is fashionable and its tail end is sold everywhere in Europe for about £6 a pound.

Seeking, as lawyers say, further and better particulars, I have read that the tails have long been prized by the Venetians, but around most of the Mediterranean it was only those huge heads that were used, for making fish soup. In Spain today, the heads may still be bought separately for this purpose, and inevitably – since the Spaniards love their fish small (and often illegally undersized) – there is a demand for little monkfish, known as *rapecitos*.

It was while staying in southern France last year that, instructed to buy some monkfish (*lotte*) in the local Carrefour supermarket, I saw, alongside the pile of gleaming fish tails, a mound of what was labelled as *foie de lotte*. Unable to resist this unheard-of delicacy, I bought the liver and we sautéed it briefly in butter and mixed it with salad leaves. Our host pronounced it to be so good that he said he would recommend it should be served on toast as a savoury at the London club of which he was chairman.

I cannot claim to be a great fan of monkfish. It has the advantage, I know, of having only one bone, its flesh is firm and it goes well with a variety of flavours. But its tail also has a membrane which takes some removing, and the reason it is said to be so good with garlic, herbs, tomatoes, mushrooms, olives, etc, is that it doesn't taste of much without some sort of assistance. Recently, I tried monkfish baked in a sauce of thickened fish stock and saffron, which was delicious, but the dish was only as good as the sauce that went with it. Larousse calls this fish 'somewhat tasteless', and Rick Stein is none too polite about its flavour. A few days old and it can be reminiscent of cotton wool; Stein likens it to India rubber.

It may be that I have never eaten monkfish straight from the sea, thinly sliced and cooked in olive oil over charcoal, which some people get very excited about. Others advise stuffing the fish with garlic and roasting it in the oven, like a leg of lamb. But I think I would rather have the lamb, and at around half the price.

While on the subject of ugly fish, John Dory comes readily to mind. I cannot really believe its name is a corruption of *jaune dorée* (who could have thought of this weird-looking, mottled grey fish as gilded yellow?), and anyway the French call it *Saint-Pierre*, after the thumb marks (similar to last month's haddock) of St Peter, made when he held the fish to extract a coin from its mouth to pay his and Jesus's taxes.

Once you have got rid of the outsize head and various fins, the fillets of John Dory may be rather small but, grilled or fried, they have an excellent flavour. There is an old Devon recipe which involves frying the fillets, skin side up, having dipped them in seasoned flour. Chopped herbs and lemon juice are added and the fish should then be simmered in cider and cream. Despite its looks, this is a proper fish, without the slightly ersatz quality of that other uncouth fish of uncertain name.

If the most expensive fish are the best fish, and are best simply cooked, the monkfish is, in my view, overpriced, because it needs sauces and strong flavours. If only some enterprising fishmonger would offer monkfish liver for sale.

Hake

Why, I wonder, is a fish revered in one European country yet largely ignored in others? As a fish of the Atlantic, and other cold waters, hake is little known in exclusively Mediterranean countries. Nor is it hugely popular in France, where it is called by one of three names – *merlu*, *merluche*, *colin* – suggesting that the French are unsure about it. Hake is certainly available here, but a lot of the British catch is sold to the country which really can't get enough of it. This, of course, is Spain, where hake (*merluza*) is the national fish.

When one considers that the Spaniards eat about four times more fish per head than we do, the question arises whether or not there is enough hake in European waters to satisfy this enormous demand. According to the Marine

Conservation Society, there isn't. Hake stocks are 'outside safe biological limits and overfished'. Many people have little respect for the practices of Spanish fishermen, assuming that they will go on hoovering hake from the seas around Europe until the stocks collapse irretrievably. It is not, of course, in Spain's interests to kill off this source of supply, and the TAC (Total Allowable Catch) has not in fact varied much over the past two years (in the North Sea it has been doubled). At the same time, Spanish boats go farther afield to meet the demand for hake. There are fisheries in the Atlantic off the north African coast, off Namibia, and in South America off Chile. Much of it is sold frozen in packs, allowing the supermarket shopper to choose from hake steaks, hake centre cuts, hake tail pieces, hake fillets with skin, hake fillets without skin.

When it comes to cooking hake it is important that the fish be really fresh. Those who have tried hake and not thought much of it will probably have noted that the flesh was soft and a bit 'cottonwoolly'. Hake will not be in prime condition for long, but while the flesh remains firm, a hake steak, taken from the middle of the fish where there will be less bone, is a very fine thing. This is a favourite among the Spanish, who will then cook it in a variety of ways.

Merluza a la Gallega (as they do it in Galicia) will be found on countless menus all over the country. The fish steaks are baked in olive oil, chopped garlic and quite a lot of paprika, and eaten with boiled potatoes. In another Iberian recipe, which I also enjoy, the fish is dusted with flour, dipped in egg, fried and eaten with melted butter and capers. Following a piece I wrote on clams, I have now learned that hake and clams are popular together, especially in the Basque country, in a dish known as *merluza en salsa verde*. The green of the sauce comes purely from the use of a lot of chopped parsley, stirred into a pan with butter, olive oil, garlic, fennel seeds and a little flour. White wine and fish stock are then added together with clams in the shell, a few peas and some previously fried hake steaks.

In France, when you can find hake on a menu, it tends to be grilled and served up with a *sauce rémoulade* or hollandaise, or a purée of sorrel. The French may be less than enthusiastic about the fish because they deem it inferior to cod, to which it is related. I think hake certainly ranks with cod, and is greatly superior to other members of the cod family, such as pollack (suitable for fish pie, and not bad when smoked), ling and coley. If you come across small hake, which may be called pin hake, they are delicious fried in very hot oil. Even smaller specimens, probably of illegal size, are offered in Spain, in Andalusia under the name of *pijotas*. Another Spanish delicacy to look out for is known as *kokotxas*, which are hake chins, delicately flavoured when fried with breadcrumbs or stewed in stock with paprika.

I like to cook one or two extra hake steaks to eat cold in a salad the following day. The flesh should be flaked and combined with lettuce, spring onions, capers and French dressing. With a few prawns, this makes a very acceptable dish for a summer lunch. So too does the *pudin de merluza* for which Penelope Casas gives the recipe in *The Foods and Wines of Spain*. It is a sort of fish loaf or hake cake, made with bread soaked in the liquid which has cooked the fish, tomato sauce, chopped pimiento and parsley, eggs and cream. The mixture is then packed into a mould and cooked slowly in a pan of water. When cold and with mayonnaise, it makes perfect eating under a Spanish sun, accompanied by lots of pink wine.

It may be while the British have been taking all those holidays in Spain that they have discovered the delights of eating hake, which are now more often sold by British fishmongers. Many of them are caught off the Devon coasts.

Quail

I wonder whether or not the US vice-president, Dick Cheney, will eat quail again after the shooting incident in south Texas in February 2006, when he ignored the most basic safety rules in shooting at his intended target while unable to see that an elderly gentleman was in his line of fire. The birds that Mr Cheney was trying to shoot would have been either scaled or bobwhite quail, both species which take to the air only reluctantly, when put up by 'bird dogs'. They never fly very far or very high, making Mr Cheney's negligence – he was apparently firing into a low, late-afternoon sun – the more culpable.

No quail are shot in this country, where a summer visitor, *Coturnix coturnix* (common quail) is the only one to be seen in the wild, and only in southern England. I have spotted a pair on the Wiltshire downs, and heard the male's strange staccato call which, according to my bird book, is a trisyllabic noise approximating to the words 'wet my lips'. Most of us, though, will have to be content to wet our lips in anticipation of a farmed quail – unless one is lucky enough to be offered a wild bird on some Mediterranean menu.

The birds are very popular in Greece, where they are either shot over pointers or netted, a practice made illegal in England almost a century ago. The Greeks traditionally wrap their quail in vine leaves, having first rubbed a mixture of honey, lemon, thyme and olive oil into the skin, and roast them in a medium oven for 20-30 minutes. In another Greek recipe the quail are stuffed with feta cheese and fenugreek before being cooked in the oven with black olives, pine nuts, crushed juniper berries and breadcrumbs.

The section on quail in Larousse is worth reading: more than 40 recipes, together with illustrations of wonderfully absurd dishes such as boned and stuffed quail in frilly paper cases with jelly and grapes, or in a nest of straw potatoes. The recipe for *chaud-froid* of quail requires the cook to 'bone ten quail and stuff with a game forcemeat. In the middle of the forcemeat put a piece of uncooked foie gras studded with a piece of truffle, seasoned with salt and spices and sprinkled with brandy. Reshape the quail, wrap each in a piece of muslin... Put these into a sauté pan on a foundation of fresh bacon rinds, carrots and onions... Cover the birds with their bones and trimmings, previously tossed in butter...' And there is much more.

But there are simpler ways. In one recipe from Larousse, for quail *petit-duc*, the birds are split down the back and flattened, sprinkled with salt, paprika and butter and grilled. Mushrooms dotted with grated horseradish and a sauce of game stock and Madeira are recommended with the quail – delicious when I tried it, with mashed potato to soak up the juices.

Nigel Slater, a great fan of quail simply cooked, writes in his *Real Cooking*: 'Hot from the grill, rubbed with spices and mustard and its brittle bones cooked to a crisp, the quail is a small orgy of sweet flesh and spicy juices. Quail is finger food and the finest feast of all for those who enjoy eating with their hands.' To chew on a grilled quail's leg which has first been marinaded in lemon juice, olive oil and crushed garlic, in an Andalusian tapas bar with a glass of manzanilla, is one of life's pleasures – but beware of the error I once made, ordering *callos* which, so close to the French word *cailles*, I assumed were quail. (*Codorniz* is the Spanish for quail; *callos* are tripe.)

Another excellent Spanish dish combines beans (lima, cannellini, borlotti), tomatoes, onion, garlic and cubes of bacon and chorizo with whole quail, first salted and browned on all sides in very hot oil before being cooked with the rest of the ingredients. Instead of beans, a risotto also goes well with roast quail, which may be wrapped in bacon rashers rather than vine leaves (the birds were sometimes put in a pig's caul in the nineteenth century). Mrs Jaffrey is in favour of using quail in a *moghlai* dish (with onions, ginger, garlic, cumin and other spices) as an alternative to chicken.

And then there are the ubiquitous quail's eggs. I am not very enthusiastic about hard-boiled eggs, with or without celery or some spicier salt. But I have recently come across the eggs boiled to a *mollet* firmness and added to a *niçoise* salad. Best of all, I think, is a sort of quail's eggs Benedict: they are poached briefly and placed on blinis, together with a warm hollandaise sauce. Three or four would make a perfect Sunday breakfast.

 Since quail sold in this country are all farmed and oven-ready, ageing and hanging are irrelevant. Most people can manage two as a main course.

Sardines

O n leave in the foothills of the Himalayas, an Indian
army officer and sportsman wrote in 1865: 'Unless
I shoot something or other, I shall have to fall back on
biscuits and sardines.' The canning of food, which had
begun in the early part of the century, was very welcome to
soldiers serving overseas who would rather leave the local
produce to the natives; and tinned sardines were a
particular favourite of the Raj. Sardines on toast were
regularly on the menu at the club, to be eaten as a savoury
after trifle or Bakewell tart and custard.

According to Felipe Fernandez-Armesto's invaluable
book, *Food: A History*, 50 million tins of sardines were
being produced annually on the west coast of France in the
1880s. Cornwall, too, was developing a successful

industry, canning the larger or adult sardines known as pilchards. Huge shoals were caught in seine nets off the coast, between July and December, then gutted and salted and stored in barrels in fish cellars. (One of these old granite buildings on the north coast was converted into flats a few years ago by the National Trust.) Much of the oil pressed from the fish was sold to the Royal Navy, and waste fish – contemporary accounts mention the appalling smell – went on to the land as a form of manure.

Then something, or rather two things, happened to the pilchards. The shoals stopped visiting the Cornish coast in such vast numbers, and there was no longer the demand for them in this country. We British prefer our sardines to be called by that name; there is something distinctly unappetising about the word pilchard, which, for some reason, puts me in mind of seedy seaside boarding houses. The word is not known to any of the European languages. Italy had always provided the principal market for Cornish pilchards, and that is where the bulk of them have gone in recent years.

But now, as the marketing men say, the product has been rebranded, and pilchards have become 'Cornish sardines' (which they were sometimes called in the nineteenth century). We may imagine barbecuing them fresh in some rocky cove – not so different from the idea of cooking them on a beach in the Algarve – and suddenly the stigma of the pilchard is gone for ever.

The reputation of the tinned sardine, however, is secure. The best are said to come from France – some shippers apparently declare vintages for them – but the Portuguese and Spanish ones are not to be sniffed at. In his *Real Fast Food*, Nigel Slater, for whom tinned sardines are comfort food, lists several ideas for sardine butter (mash up the fish, having poured away the oil, with an equal quantity of butter and a little lemon juice) and sardine sandwiches. I like his suggestion of grilling the sardines briefly with a coating of mustard and eating them with thick slices of brown bread. They may also be put on fingers of fried bread, adding a sauce made with egg yolks, butter, mustard and vinegar.

Sardines, whether canned or fresh, are said to be rich in calcium and therefore good for the bones. When fresh, they are probably best simply grilled or cooked on one of those griddles known in Spain as *planchas*. Before grilling or frying, it is a good idea, and a fairly easy job, to 'butterfly' the fish, cutting along the belly to the tail, pulling out the guts and, when the fish is opened out, the backbone. Following a Rick Stein recipe, dip the sardines in flour, then a beaten egg and finally a mixture of breadcrumbs, grated Parmesan cheese and parsley before deep-frying them. Or wrap them in smoked streaky bacon rashers and bake in the oven.

Sardines also lend themselves to an *escabeche*, where they are first briefly fried in olive oil, then marinated in a mixture, which has been boiled and simmered, of red wine vinegar, dried chillies, onion, garlic, fennel seeds and grated orange peel. In Cornwall one might come across Stargazey pie, where the fresh pilchards are baked in a shallow dish and have their heads poking up through the pastry. From Morocco comes a recipe for butterflied sardines made into a sandwich filled with crushed garlic, cumin seeds and coriander leaves. Sounds delicious, but for the moment I think I shall go to the larder, open a tin of French sardines which have been smoked over beechwood and enjoy them with thick buttered toast.

The long-lingering taste of tinned sardines can be mitigated by drinking a glass or two of Champagne with them.

Mackerel

The childhood memories are clear: a small fishing-boat rocks in the Atlantic swell off the north Cornish coast, and the line, stretching not far below the surface and grasped expectantly, is definitely twitching. There is at least one mackerel on the end, but how many more? As the line is drawn to the boat and hauled from the water with help from the fisherman, each of the six hooks has a beautiful, blue-green and silvery fish writhing on it – a full house! An excited struggle ensues, as everyone aboard tries to grab the fish, wriggling and slippery, from the bottom of the boat and throw them into the fish box. And then the line, 'baited' with coloured elastic bands, goes down again.

Of course, we would eat the mackerel the same day, or possibly for breakfast the following morning, split open, with the backbone removed, sprinkled with flour and fried. A mackerel as fresh as this is almost indescribably delicious – oily, meaty, yet delicate in flavour. I have not been out fishing for mackerel for a few years, since my own children grew up, but in Cornwall each year we can always buy mackerel which have been locally caught the day before.

Apparently, mackerel contain more fatty matter than any other fish, which makes it the more important that they be eaten fresh. Away from the coast, really fresh mackerel are not easy to find, but they can be identified, as can other fish, by their glossy skins and the brightness of their eyes. Rick Stein offers the intelligence that the larger winter fish, caught in deep water, have better keeping qualities than the less oily small summer mackerel.

There is, however, no particular season for mackerel. They are said to spawn in spring and summer, yet also to be at their best in April, which is slightly confusing. A more useful tip is to look out for the male fish's soft roes, which should be briefly poached in water, butter and lemon juice. It is, of course, reassuring to know that by eating mackerel, or any other oily fish, one is reducing the risk of heart disease, while at the same time enjoying one of the cheapest fish around. According to an eighteenth-century diary, mackerel were then selling at 'twopence' each in the Weymouth market; and they can still be had for less than £2 a pound.

Grilling this fish whole is probably the easiest and one of the best methods of cooking it. Nigel Slater, in his *Real Fast Food*, goes so far as to say that grilled mackerel 'undergoes the most magical transformation... its flesh becoming rich and sweet, taking on a smoky note from the skin as it chars'. Having slashed the skin a couple of times on each side, squeeze the juice of half a lemon over it and grill under a high heat. When a mackerel is filleted – a fairly simple operation once you have been shown how to do it – a combination of prepared mustard, lemon juice and olive oil may be brushed over the fillets before grilling or cooking in the oven.

As an improvement on this, I must mention the recipe for one of the finest sauces to be found in Elizabeth David's *French Provincial Cooking*. This – the page is permanently marked in my paperback copy of the book – consists of two egg yolks, a teaspoon of Dijon mustard, salt, pepper, a few drops of vinegar and plenty of chopped parsley and any other herbs available. Two ounces of melted butter are then added slowly, and the sauce is made. Mrs David recommends poaching the fish in a *court-bouillon* before filleting and skinning it; the dish, from Brittany, is known as *maquereau à la façon de Quimper*.

Some reference should be made to the gooseberry sauce which is supposed to go so well with mackerel – acidity meeting oiliness – but I prefer my fish without fruit. (For those who like the idea, try rhubarb, too.) I am happier marinating *maquereau au vin blanc*, with sliced onion and carrot and herbs, adding vinegar, garlic and chilli to sharpen it up.

Smoked mackerel, which has usually been cooked in hot smoke, is quite ordinary in my view; better when cold-smoked, like smoked salmon. Most appealing, however, are thin slices of the freshest raw mackerel, as part of a sashimi of raw fish, to which my daughter introduced me in Japan. With a dipping sauce of soy, grated ginger, juice and zest of lime, and a little of that fiery green horseradish called wasabi on the side, this makes an outstanding starter. But it might shock a Cornish fisherman.

Almost always sold as a whole fish, a fresh mackerel can be readily identified. It should not be bought if its eyes are dull and sunken, and its gills have gone a dark red-brown.

Prawns

The proliferating number and variety of uncooked prawns to be found in the shops put me in mind of the words of the foul-mouthed Australian, Barry McKenzie, in the Barry Humphries/Nicholas Garland strip cartoon which used to run in *Private Eye,* 'Don't come the raw prawn with me, sport.' The problem with most raw prawns, which have been imported, usually farmed and frozen, is that they lose flavour when thawed and are then likely to be boiled in fresh, not sea, water. Those monster prawns from Sri Lanka and off the Mozambique coast which are sold fresh can be delicious when grilled or barbecued, but they do cost about £15 per pound, including the shell and huge head.

The best-value prawns, and often the best-flavoured, are those which have been fished from the North Atlantic, cooked in sea water and frozen at sea, then sold with their heads and shells on (at around £1.50 per pint). These have the additional advantage that the shells may be used in making soups and sauces or – which often happens in our house – boiled up and fed to the chickens. A delicious bisque can be made with chopped vegetables (carrot, onion, celery), garlic, wine, tomatoes, rice and stock, all stewed with the prawn shells, then passed through a blender and a sieve before adding cream.

There is nothing wrong with the now derided prawn cocktail, provided the mayonnaise is good; and it can be improved by adding crushed garlic or grated horseradish and Tabasco sauce in place of tomato ketchup. Rice is a very good accompaniment for prawns, briefly sautéed, perhaps, in butter, cream and Pernod, with lemon juice and nutmeg, or – a great favourite since I first started going to Indian restaurants – cooked in spices with spinach. Prawns *piri-piri*, with a chilli sauce, is a dish popular in Portugal and southern Africa. Rowley Leigh produced an excellent and simple recipe for prawn pilaff a few years ago in the *Sunday Telegraph* magazine (no longer worth reading since someone took the insane decision to replace him). This is best made in a wok, with oil, butter and softened onion, to which you add basmati rice, water, frozen peas and sweetcorn, then the cooked prawns at the end.

In fact, Leigh called this dish shrimp pilaff, possibly because it would be more recognisable to Americans, for whom all prawns are shrimps or, rather, shrimp. Anyone who has fished for these crustaceans on the coasts of Britain will immediately be able to distinguish between a shrimp, an opaque pale grey when caught in a net at low tide at the sea's edge, and the more transparent and larger prawn, usually found in rock pools feeding on seaweed. And they are still fun to catch; the excitement of seeing the little creatures flicking about in the bottom of the net remains with me from childhood.

Prawn terminology gets more complicated when you move on to the subject of Dublin Bay prawns. These have claws and are now more generally known, and sold, as langoustines, many of them caught in Scottish waters where they are simply called prawns or – to add to the confusion – Norway lobsters. When in Spain you might think that the *langostinos* on the menu would be langoustines, but they are not. They are large prawns, also called *gambas*, and the bigger red-shelled ones are *carabineros*. If you want Dublin Bay prawns in Spain, ask for *cigalas*. In Italy they are called *scampi*, but do not expect the pub-grub scampi and chips to have much to do with the real thing. By whatever name, the clawed creatures are delectably sweet, requiring the briefest of cooking, whether boiled and eaten with mayonnaise or grilled with butter, and their season is starting this month.

It is but a small step, in size and appearance, from langoustines to freshwater crayfish (*écrevisses*), which I have caught in our stream at home. They are American imports, escapees from a farm in the upper reaches of the Wiltshire Avon, and they are apparently, as is the way with Americans, using their superior strength to crush the smaller indigenous species. The good news is that they come into our shallow stream in October – which is their mating season, I am told – and can be seen scuttling in and out of little mud caves in the stream bank. They are easily caught, the claws as well as the tails are large enough to be worth eating, and three or four will make a very acceptable first course for supper. We are already looking forward to this year's autumn crayfish run.

The prawns caught in northern waters, which are often sold with their shells on, are a good source of vitamin B12 as well as other vitamins. Eat the prawns in their shells (having removed heads and tails) and they will be even more nutritious. Unless shrimps are to be potted, they are also even tastier with shells intact.

Whitebait

A n Indian friend with whom I was staying in the Nilgiri
Hills asked what had happened to the whitebait which
he used to enjoy years ago in England, during his time at
Cambridge. In those far-off days, whitebait appeared on
restaurant or pub menus as a starter with the same frequency
as egg mayonnaise or half an avocado pear. Tiny fish known
as whiting in Tamil Nadu made very good whitebait, he said,
and I had seen something similar in Kerala (there called
mullet) pulled from the sea in those 'Chinese' fishing nets
introduced from the Far East in the fourteenth century. Deep-
fried whitebait, using whatever fish they may be, and dusted
with flour and chilli powder, make a popular dish in the clubs
of south India – where steak and kidney pie is still to be
found on the menu as often as chicken biryani.

The traditionally English whitebait, however, are likely to come frozen from Holland these days. Time was when shoals of whitebait (the fry of sprats and herring, although they were once thought to be a distinct species) swarmed around the Thames estuary and were as popular as oysters in the taverns of the South East. Annual whitebait dinners were first held in Dagenham on the Essex shore in the eighteenth century, and to one of these Pitt was invited as prime minister. The occasions became popular with government ministers and were later transferred to Greenwich (handier for the House of Commons), where they were held regularly until the 1890s.

Today, the tradition survives in the whitebait dinner held every autumn by the Saints and Sinners Club at the Trafalgar Tavern, but the baby fishes will probably have been brought from off the Dutch coast. Several other countries outside Europe, such as India and Japan, have their own versions of whitebait. In New Zealand, where the same name is used and the season is anticipated with enthusiasm as it once was in England, the fish consist of the young of three species unheard of in this country but helpfully identified on the internet as inanga, koaro and banded kokopu.

As one might have guessed, whitebait have long been used as bait fish; coarse fishermen will get a bag of sprats, for next to nothing, from a fishmonger's stall at the end of the day. On their own, and when larger than whitebait size, sprats (garvies in Scotland) fried in flour or in batter can be very appetising; and smoked sprats are well worth adding to a smoked fish platter. (The Norwegian sprats known as brisling which used to be canned and sold as Skippers before World War II were the brainchild of a non-conformist Liberal and obsessive teetotaller called Angus Watson who was also co-proprietor of *The Spectator*.)

Although there is really only one way to cook whitebait, there are minor variations, or differences of opinion, in the recommended preparation and frying of them. Some wash the fish in water before tossing them in seasoned flour in a plastic bag, while the two supreme fish cookery writers, Jane Grigson and Rick Stein, advise dipping them first in milk, then in flour. Plain flour seems to be favourite, though it can be mixed with cornflour.

The whitebait should then be fried in very hot vegetable oil – for about one and a half minutes in my recent experience – either in a deep pan with a basket or in a wok. If the fish are not crisp enough when removed from the heat, pat them dry before returning them briefly to the pan, keeping the oil as hot as possible. I have heard of a tomato, onion and caper salsa being served with whitebait, but I think they need no more than lemon juice and a shake of cayenne pepper. They may also be fried in batter as part of a *fritto misto*.

No one seems to have an explanation for the disappearance of the shoals of baby sprats and herring from the mouth of the Thames estuary. Perhaps it has something to with the pollution of the river in the recent past or with the fact that too few fish were allowed to grow old enough to reproduce in large numbers. The good news is that a fishmonger in Southend, where a whitebait festival used to be held every year, told me recently that a local fisherman, off Burnham-on-Crouch, had just made his first big catch of whitebait in four years. Perhaps they are on their way back.

Bags of frozen whitebait can be bought from Martin's Seafresh in Cornwall (see page 159). If you happen to come across sand-eels, they may be cooked as whitebait.

Pigeon

There never seems to be any shortage of pigeons. Whether feeding in a field of corn or rape by day, or coming into woodland at dusk, they are always around. Depending on the weather and the time of day, you may have to wait a while but, as William Douglas-Home once wrote in a memorable article for *The Field* on pigeon-shooting, 'they always turn up in the end'. They may be shot over decoys in spring and summer or from the shelter of trees on a winter's afternoon; with no close season there should always be a plentiful supply for the table.

These, of course, are wood pigeons. In addition, and especially in France, there are 'farmed' pigeons or squabs raised for meat, rather as they used to be in dovecotes in England, to provide food for the medieval lord of the manor when cattle could not be fed through the winter. Many dovecotes are works of art, and not only in Europe. I am thinking of one I have seen in Seringapatam, southern India, and of those exotic structures attached to the walls of palaces in Turkey, because in the pre-Muslim era the Turks believed that a person's soul was carried by pigeons to the gods. Pigeons were used to take messages during the Siege of Paris in 1870-1871, and a military pigeon-house was built in the French city of Albi during World War I for those birds employed to carry the 'pigeon post'.

When the French keep pigeons today, they will be for racing or for the pot. If you are offered a whole roast pigeon in France, the chances are it will be a young reared bird, known as *un pigeonneau*. This is usually a more succulent, more tender bird than a wood pigeon, and with meat on the legs which is worth eating. The wild pigeons are more likely to be casseroled, as in the *salmis de palombes* which I have eaten in the French Basque country, where these migrant birds are shot and netted in large numbers as they pass through the western Pyrenees.

Such a *salmis* is often made by part-cooking the whole bird, then cutting off and reserving the breasts while a sauce is made from the legs and carcass, together with red wine, garlic, juniper berries, thyme and a *beurre manié*.

Redcurrant jelly and port may also be added, while the pigeon's bones are discarded. A French domestic pigeon might be stuffed with garlic and anchovies, roasted with bacon and eaten with a sauce of reduced white wine and stock, plus, according to one French recipe, a large white turnip '*enrobé de lard et clouté de pignons* [studded with pine nuts]'. *Très amusant.*

Since these reared birds are seldom for sale in England, we must find something else to do, apart from making a *salmis*, with our wood pigeons. It is important that they be young birds. Colin McKelvie, in his introductory notes to that excellent book of European recipes, *Good Game*, opines that, 'an old pigeon can be tougher than almost anything else old'. That book recommends grilling pigeons which have been marinated overnight in port, red wine, oil and orange (zest and juice); casseroling them with tomatoes, green olives and white wine; and baking them, split in half and devilled. When the whole bird is cooked, beware of small, sharp bones.

In a French recipe from the Landes which I have just tried, the wild birds are braised in butter for half an hour or so, then cut in half and reheated on a bed of puréed artichoke hearts, together with the pigeons' chopped-up liver and a gravy made from the buttery juices, white wine, brandy and lemon juice. Unfortunately, my pigeons had lost their livers, but the dish was still delicious. I have enjoyed pigeon breasts simply fried for breakfast, with eggs and bacon – very sustaining before a day's shooting. And if the birds are past their youthful best, their breasts can be made into an excellent pâté.

The Moroccans do a sort of pigeon pie called *bestilla*, a dish which they also bequeathed to southern Spain when they were expelled from the peninsula in the fifteenth century. The traditional English pigeon pie includes stewing steak, onions, mushrooms and almost anything else that seems suitable. Which reminds me that this is, or that it used to be, the season for rook pie, once the young birds have fledged. The breasts are layered with pieces of rump steak, covered with a strong stock and a pastry crust. Having never tried rook, however, I am happy to stick with pigeon.

A bird that has been recently shot should have its crop emptied, its head hung downwards and bled so that the flesh will not be too dark. Once plucked and drawn, look for the plumpest breasts and pale-coloured legs.

Sole

Sole Bay, I had always assumed, was where the Dover soles came from which I have often bought on the Suffolk coast at Aldeburgh. This may well be so, but I have only recently learnt that the name Sole Bay has nothing to do with the fish. Actually, it is a Suffolk-speak contraction of Southwold Bay, where the British fleet fought the Dutch to an inconclusive draw in 1672. (For this information I am indebted to the chairman of Adnams, which illustrates the Battle of Sole Bay on the labels of its fine Broadside beer.)

Some of the best Dover soles, however, do come out of the North Sea, rather than from the English Channel, having acquired their name from the time when they were landed at Dover for delivery to the capital. (Surprisingly, the French are prepared to use the name, even when the fish come from the Bay of Biscay, while the Irish, having changed most English names, call them black soles.) The soles of Suffolk that I have most enjoyed have been 'slips', which weigh less than eight ounces and are cheaper per pound than the larger fish. One potential problem with a large Dover sole is that, if overcooked, its flesh can become dry and a bit rubbery; another, at least for those living in London, is its price. I was astonished to find earlier in the year, having bought a perfectly fresh, 16-ounce sole in Devizes for £5.60, that the same-sized fish from Selfridges in Oxford Street would cost £14.50. I know that Dover sole is one of the most highly prized white fish, but that is ridiculous.

Perhaps this absurd price difference can be partly explained by the fashion for eating Dover sole in smart London houses and restaurants, which goes back many years. In the inter-war period fillets of sole, inevitably smothered in some rich and highly flavoured sauce which was liable to kill the sweet and delicate flavour of the fish, were seldom off the menu. I have a copy of *Madame Prunier's Fish Cookery Book*, in which she lists no fewer than 124 recipes for sole, or rather 124 different sauces, most of which seem to involve lobster or other shellfish, truffles, mushrooms, cheese, wine and cream. One particularly unappealing idea, combining the fried fillets with aubergines, red peppers, stewed tomatoes and garlic, is called *sole Alphonse XIII*, presumably in honour of the previous Spanish king – and he wasn't much of a success either. A few of the names – *sole Veronique* (which Madame Prunier strangely omits to mention), *sole Walewska*, *sole Cubat* – I remember from Wheeler's restaurants in the 1960s, but I don't suppose they are to be found today. Larousse has photographs of some of these extravagant concoctions.

Nowadays, it seems to be accepted that the best way with sole is to grill it on the bone with butter, before adding lemon juice, chopped parsley and some more, slightly burnt butter – and, if you insist, a few capers or chopped anchovies. Constance Spry, not best known for the simplicity of her recipes, writes that one of the best fish she ever had was a plainly grilled sole which had just been landed at some Scottish port. 'It had a sweetness of nuts, tasted of the sea, and was so Lucullean a dish that it needed no frills of any sort or kind, though it was bedewed with fresh butter cooked to a golden brown.' Pushing the hyperbole aside, one knows what she meant.

Sole may also be fried (*meunière*), and I am prepared to accept it cooked in the oven, with shallots and white wine (*Bercy*) or with mussels, mussel stock and parsley butter (*Normande*) or, just occasionally, baked in cream with lemon juice, cayenne pepper and parsley. But no silly sauces, which belong to the era of ladies with cigarette holders and men sporting spats. We may regret its passing, but it is past.

Lemon sole, on the other hand, may benefit from something like a sorrel sauce. Its flesh is soft and is perfectly all right on its own, but nevertheless it is a dull fish. However, if you make the mistake of going to an expensive London fishmonger, you may have to pay as much for it as for the infinitely superior Dover sole bought in Wiltshire. In my view, megrim sole has a better flavour than lemon sole, but it is also known as whiff, which is slightly off-putting. About the other soles – Torbay, witch and sand – I am not entirely clear. One of them may be an alternative name for another; although I hesitate to say this, it is hard to know which is witch.

Lemon sole has its merits, and its fans, but I would always rather save up for a Dover sole, preferably the small 'slips' which are not that expensive. Best eaten on the bone.

Squid

In marine lore, giant squid are seen as the monsters of the deep. I remember being told that when one had coiled a tentacle around a fishing boat off the Azores and the fisherman had hacked it off, it was estimated from the piece of tentacle which he brought back to port that it would have had a total length of some 27 feet. The overall length of a giant squid can apparently reach 60 feet. At the other end of the squid scale are the minuscule little babies, known as *chopitos* in southern Spain, which are fried in batter and eaten whole; about 30 of them will provide a reasonable first course.

An extraordinary creature is this cephalopod, a word meaning head-footed and referring to the way in which its arms and tentacles, like those of the octopus and cuttlefish, sprout directly from its head. (If anyone wants to be excessively well informed on the subject, my edition of the *Encyclopaedia Britannica* devotes no less than 17 of its pages to cephalopoda.) The best way to learn about squid is to take a knife and cut one up, ready for the pan or pot. While to some people this might be an unpleasant task, I have to say that I find it rather satisfying. The head and tentacles are easily detached from the body, then the eyes, the ink bags and a little crusty piece within the tentacles are removed. (I am grateful to Elizabeth David for the information that this last object, according to Dumas, is '*non pas un nez mais l'anus au milieu du visage*'.) The fins should be cut from the body and all the thin purplish membrane peeled off. The gunge is easily squeezed from the cone-shaped body, and the transparent spine bone removed; this is a thing of beauty, resembling a delicate quill pen. Then, if you insist, you can cut the body into rings, but don't throw away the fins or tentacles.

A lot of people think of squid only as fried calamari rings, and pretty tasteless they can be, often large, overcooked, dried up and unpleasantly chewy. But when flash-fried, together with the tentacles, in a little olive oil, with lemon juice and pepper, they can taste quite different. The body of the squid may also be cut once down the side and flattened out, then lightly scored into diamond patterns with a knife and cut into pieces about three inches square. When put into a very hot pan and briefly fried, they will curl up and look rather like miniature hand grenades. With some chopped red chilli, the flavour can be fairly explosive, too.

The important thing, of course, is not to overcook squid when frying it. On the other hand, it can be stewed slowly in, say, red wine, with onions, garlic and herbs. The classic Spanish dish of *calamares en su tinta* is made with tomatoes, parsley, garlic, wine and the fish's ink (which can be bought separately), all cooked slowly with the squid for an hour or more. Since the body of the squid is the perfect shape for stuffing, that is often what is done with it. Chopped raw ham is a good ingredient, also breadcrumbs or hard-boiled egg, in addition to onion, garlic and parsley. It is a good idea to skewer the stuffed squid with a toothpick before cooking, first browned in hot oil, then casseroled slowly with a splash or two of sherry at the end.

Of the other two members of the cephalopod family – octopus and cuttlefish – I know little. In northern Italy, they stew all three together, and I have been fascinated to see boxes of cuttlefish, covered in ink, in the Venice fish market by the Rialto Bridge. In Galicia, northern Spain, I have seen octopus boiled in metal drums and have eaten them from wooden bowls. But my most vivid memory of octopus was eating them at a village festival in Japan, fried in balls of batter, and served from a street stall by our daughter.

I am happy to stay with squid, however, which were once almost impossible to find in this country, but are now readily available. The little squid which I buy in our local Waitrose supermarket are ideal for searing in a pan with olive oil, garlic, paprika and lemon juice. Half a dozen of them with salad make a good supper, and cost less than a pound.

As with a number of other fish, so it is with the cephalopods – squid, octopus and cuttlefish: smaller is better, in this case because they are not so likely to be rubbery if overcooked.

Tuna

A few years before his assassination in 1908, King Carlos of Portugal published a book on the tuna, its distribution and the various species of the fish. I am not aware of any other reigning monarch having written a book on fish, and it may have been Carlos's most important legacy.

In those days, the English name for tuna was tunny, and it is not entirely clear why or when it was changed to tuna. The word may be an import from the United States, since that is the Spanish-American word for the Pacific species of the fish caught off the California coast. From European waters we are familiar with the yellow-fin and blue-fin tuna, while the albacore and skipjack are inferior species often used for canning.

To those who revile Spanish fishermen, it is worth pointing out that they are environmentally correct in their catching of tuna on long lines, whereas the drift-nets more often used from British boats may trap dolphins as well as tuna. Nor will the drift-netted fish always be in prime condition: if bruised and damaged by being thrown around in a huge net, they will have to be sold for processing.

A great deal more damage is presumably done to the tuna flesh in the killing rituals which take place every year in Sicily. In spring, the fish gather in shoals and migrate inshore to breed. They are then trapped in netted enclosures, which are lifted to the surface to enable the Sicilians to gaff and club them to death in a brutal and bloody manner reminiscent of a Mafia revenge killing.

In spite of today's fashion for fresh, often 'seared', tuna, the majority of the fish caught are canned, in oil or brine. It was not so many years ago that tuna (or rather, tunny) was offered in restaurants only as part of an *hors d'oeuvre*. Mrs Beeton and Constance Spry give one recipe each – the preserved tuna, combined with mayonnaise, is mixed with grapefruit (Beeton) or cucumber (Spry). Other countries have, of course, done better with their cans of tuna – the French with *salade niçoise* and the Italians with *vitello tonnato*. This delicious Mediterranean example of surf 'n turf needs a mayonnaise made with the addition of tuna, anchovy fillets and capers all pounded together and then spread over a previously cooked piece of veal and eaten cold.

In her *Italian Food*, Elizabeth David devotes several pages to dishes with tinned tuna, but there is no mention of a tuna omelette – perhaps because the Italians are not very good at omelettes. In France, I have occasionally eaten the *omelette du curé* (named after a poor priest whom the famously beautiful Madame Recamier was visiting when he asked her to stay for supper), and it is well worth trying to recreate at home, using tinned or fresh tuna and a little chopped shallot.

I am not being sniffy about tinned tuna when I say that I prefer the fish fresh. A *salade niçoise* is improved by using fresh tuna steak (the fatty belly of the fish – *ventresca*, or *toro* in Japanese – is said to be the superior cut), and it would be a terrible mistake to go through life without trying raw tuna. In America and, for all I know, in London too, you can buy what is called sashimi-grade tuna, usually taken from the blue-fin which is so much in demand in Japan. I would suggest either dipping pieces of the raw fish into soy sauce flavoured with grated ginger, lime zest and lime juice, or making a *carpaccio* by slicing the tuna very thinly (easier when it is slightly frozen) and spooning over it a dressing made with the best olive oil, lemon juice, chopped capers and oregano.

When you come to sear the tuna steaks, as modern chefs so enjoy doing, beware of using too thick a piece and allowing the raw middle to stay cold and rather tasteless. Matthew Fort, in his highly enjoyable book, *Eating up Italy*, provides the helpful information that the Italians, who know their tuna, use slices no more than one centimetre thick which, having been grilled or fried quickly in olive oil over a high heat, are full of flavour and cooked through. An outstanding recipe from *Moro: The Cookbook* suggests first marinading the fish in oloroso sherry, crushed garlic and salt, then slowly frying Spanish onions to which more sherry is added. When the tuna has been cooked (in another pan) the marinade and the onion sauce are poured over it, with chopped parsley and lemon juice. *Muy rico.*

*The tuna loin, when very fresh, is suitable for slicing very thinly and eating raw (*sashimi*). Salt-cured and wind-dried slices of the fish are sold in southern Spain and called* mojama.

Chicken / Turkey

If, as I was told the other day, much of the frozen chicken and duck meat brought into this country comes from the Far East, it may be that some of us have already been exposed to the risk of contracting avian flu. But I don't suppose that this will weigh with the government when there is another major scare – a couple of chickens found to have the dreaded virus in a heavily populated part of southern England – and, with its instinct for over-reaction, the Department for Environment, Food and Rural Affairs will order that all poultry be kept indoors. When shall we be able to enjoy a free-range chicken or a free-range egg again?

Not wishing to be a Jeremiah, I would rather describe the joys of eating this remarkable domestic bird. The French like to know what sort of poultry they are getting (such as the famous *poulet de Bresse*, from Burgundy), but the most important thing is that the bird should be free-range, whether for the quality of its flesh or its eggs. And by free-range I do not mean hundreds of birds kept in a shed with a small 'pop-hole' which, in effect, allows only a tiny proportion of them to venture outside. The birds should be able to range freely on grass all day long and grow naturally; if they are also fed corn, so much the better. The fact that they may be classified as organic, according to the standards of the Soil Association, adds nothing, in my humble opinion, to their flavour, although quite a lot to their price.

When we had a house years ago in southern Spain, a local smallholder would occasionally bring to our door what he called a *pollo de campo*, which had probably never been indoors in its life. The skin and flesh had a yellowish tinge and were memorably delicious. When the meat is this good it is best eaten simply roasted, having been smeared all over with butter and perhaps had garlic and a lemon stuffed into its cavity. (The juice of the lemon can be squeezed over the bird before cooking.) Proper bread sauce is almost obligatory, made by sticking cloves into a whole onion, soaking it in warmed milk with a bay leaf, then discarding the onion and adding breadcrumbs, butter and grated nutmeg. The usual problems with bread sauce in restaurants and other people's houses are that it may be stodgy, having been made from a packet and left to congeal, and that there is never enough of it.

There are endless ways with chicken, many of which incorporate tarragon; and there is no point in pretending that all dishes are improved by paying more than £3 per pound for an organic bird. The flavours in *coq au vin* – bacon, onions, garlic, mushrooms, thyme and red wine – will lift the blandest of hens. An old boiling fowl is traditionally used for another French classic, *poule au pot*, made with wine and root vegetables, which Henri IV wanted every family in his kingdom to eat for their Sunday lunch.

A chicken leg grilled on a barbecue, the skin brushed with oil and mustard, is something to look forward to in summer. And no one should underestimate or be ashamed to admit to the pleasure of eating cold chicken with salt and Branston Pickle. Chicken livers are another favourite of mine – briefly sautéed in butter and poured over salad leaves with vinaigrette. Nigel Slater recommends combining sliced garlic, white grapes and cream with the livers.

I know there are some who prefer their chicken gently poached, with a soothing cream sauce, but I find that the stronger flavoured sauces – *ravigote*, *aïoli* – are well suited to any bird that is not being roasted. Guinea fowl, which never seems to me to have the gamey taste which is often claimed for it, goes well with *aïoli*. Be sure to cook the bird in wine or stock as the flesh tends to go dry. I would rather have a Cornish game hen (also known as Indian game) which has especially good leg meat, rather like the legs of a turkey.

The turkey is indigenous to America, where it is still shot as a game bird in some states. Our domesticated bird should also be treated as game and hung for about a week before being drawn. The flavour of a turkey will be improved, too, by having had barley in its diet and by being hand-plucked (machine plucking involves immersing the bird in water, which is likely to give the flesh an insipid taste).

When it comes to cooking the bird, which does not have to be eaten only once a year, I bear in mind the advice from my late mother-in-law, that no turkey needs more than two and a half hours in the oven. (The alternative is to cook breast and legs separately; if the breast meat crumbles when carved, it is hardly worth eating.) For me, the legs, and the parson's nose, are the best parts of the turkey, to be eaten with two stuffings – one made with apple, black pudding and the turkey liver, the other with prunes, chestnuts and celery – and, of course, a bucket of bread sauce.

The cheapest supermarket chicken will probably have had a life of no more than five weeks. Generally speaking, the more mature birds will have more flavour, particularly if they were kept free-range.

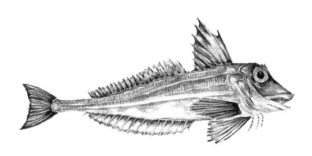

Gurnard

The gurnard is an odd fish. Known formerly as gurnet, it apparently makes a grunting sound (hence its French name, *grondin*) both in the water and when caught. The better known red gurnard (the grey is also found in British waters) has been called 'English soldier' by the Dutch, recalling their redcoat enemies. But it is, in fact, a rather foreign-looking fish, with a flat, bony head, a snout and lots of fins. It may sometimes be passed off in France as red mullet, with which it should not be confused. The quality of the gurnard's flesh, however, is a great deal better than its price would indicate, although not widely appreciated. I think of it as a West Country fish: Charles Kingsley, brought up in Devon, was a fan of gurnard, commenting that it was 'despised by deluded Cockneys'. At about a third of the cost of sea bass or bream, I would be surprised if, in a blind tasting of the three fish, the gurnard was judged to be inferior.

The fillets may be grilled or baked, possibly with a sharp sauce. Mrs Beeton bakes the fish whole, with its tail pushed into its mouth, stuffed with veal forcemeat and covered with bacon rashers. However, having recently attended a course at Rick Stein's Padstow Seafood School, gurnard is associated primarily for me with a *bouillabaisse*. Yes, I know that *bouillabaisse* is a dish which should be eaten in Marseilles – Elizabeth David has written that there is no point in making it away from the shores of the Mediterranean – but our Atlantic equivalent was pretty damn good, with the red-skinned rascasse, essential to the Provençal dish, being replaced by the red gurnard.

We gathered early in the morning at Newlyn fish market to await the daily auction. There were boxes of gurnard, many of them very small, which would be bought as bait for lobster pots. With the help of an auctioneer, our little party of prospective cooks returned to Padstow with a selection of white fish: gurnard, John Dory, monkfish, turbot. (The turbot, I thought, was a bit spoiling, since *bouillabaisse* is meant to be a fisherman's dish. The ling and tope for sale in the market might have been more appropriate.) After a sustaining late breakfast of kedgeree and fresh orange juice at the seafood school, we began to learn, under the guidance of an excellent Irish chef/tutor, how to make what he, in his soft Cavan accent, called 'boolabess'.

First came a lesson in filleting, with heads and bones being used to make stock, then a *mirepoix* of chopped onions, leeks, fennel, celery and garlic. To this, when cooked gently in olive oil, were added strips of orange zest, chopped tomatoes and red chilli, saffron, thyme, bay leaves and the stock which had been simmering for about 20 minutes.

It was now time for the student chefs to do it themselves. For the preparation and cooking we worked in pairs. I was partnered by a friend, a former military attaché and now a colonel working for the Ministry of Defence, who filleted away with admirable precision, and chopped vegetables with the sort of swift, staccato movements which presumably he had learnt on the parade ground. Glasses of white wine were passed around to aid our concentration, and the occasion became one of jolly banter and friendly rivalry – the very antithesis of the atmosphere on those demeaning Gordon Ramsay television programmes which were being shown at the time. We were in 'Heaven's Kitchen'.

So relaxed were we in our work that the man from the MoD suddenly murmured something about having to let his dog out and disappeared, just at the critical moment when the *mirepoix* was to be amalgamated with the fish stock. He returned soon enough, however, while the liquid was reducing in a large wok. We added the filleted fish and simmered everything for a few more minutes.

To keep my MoD friend at his post, I suggested that he should make the croutons (slices of French bread, fried on both sides and rubbed with garlic) while I cleaned a few mussels which were then added to the broth, together with fennel tops and a good splash of Pernod. We then threw in a few cooked prawns and spread the fried bread with *rouille* which had been helpfully prepared by our Irish tutor. The pink skin of the gurnard fillets showed up well as everything was arranged in large soup plates, and we tucked in with more white wine followed by a Provence rosé. For some reason, the conversation turned from fish to a forthcoming international football championship. Few of the England team might have appreciated what we were eating, but I'm sure that great Marseillais, Zinedine Zidane, would have approved.

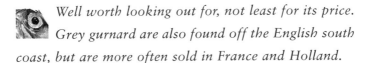 *Well worth looking out for, not least for its price. Grey gurnard are also found off the English south coast, but are more often sold in France and Holland.*

Mullet

I n France last summer, buying a couple of red mullet in the Cahors market, I asked the fishmonger who offered to clean them not to throw away the liver. With a look of some surprise – presumably he never expected a foreigner to know about this great delicacy – he then proceeded to tell me that, having grilled the *rouget* on a bed of fennel stalks over an open fire, I must pound the liver with olive oil, garlic and a little cognac so that it becomes a sauce, *pour ainsi dire*, to accompany itself. We had a memorable barbecue that evening.

Many modern recipes tell you not to remove the liver when cleaning the fish, but they do not usually recommend making it into a separate sauce. However, a mid-nineteenth-century writer on the 'Art of Dining' records that the Duke of

Portland was in the habit of buying a quantity of red mullet in Weymouth during the summer and putting 'all the livers together in a butter-boat, to avoid the chances of inequality'. Some epicures took to 'eating the flesh of the dory with the liver of the mullet', judging the mullet's flesh to be inferior.

I cannot agree with that. A really fresh mullet, grilled until the pink skin becomes brown and crisp, is a wonderful thing, redolent of the Mediterranean. (Years ago, I used to go after these fish with a speargun off the Majorcan coast, where they are called *salmonetes*; but oddly my Spanish cookery book makes no mention of them.) Rick Stein describes the taste of red mullet as 'somewhere between fish and lobster', referring also, I presume, to the firmness of the flesh which makes it so suitable for filleting and serving in a variety of ways, both hot and cold.

Mullet seems to be rather fashionable these days as a first course. A single fillet, baked or grilled, is surrounded by a tomato and basil dressing or a red pepper salsa, and the other day I had the mullet with a dollop of cod and potato *brandade* (also very fashionable, but it might have been better on its own). In a Berlin restaurant recently, the menu described a piece of mullet floating in a curried fennel cream soup, but I let that pass. Although these fish will be landed at West Country fishing ports later in the summer, they are irresistibly associated with Provence, where they are often served with tomatoes, garlic, olives and anchovy fillets, *à la Niçoise*, and can be eaten cold. More simply, they may be baked in foil or paper cases, with lemon juice and thyme. Baby mullet are delicious when floured and fried, without removing their innards, then dipped in a tartare sauce. For some obscure reason, this is known in France as *rougets à la Juive*.

If you are cooking mullet whole and unskinned, it should first be scaled (working from the tail and using the back of a knife), which is likely to make quite a mess. The scales of the grey mullet, an unrelated and often underrated fish, are larger and easier to deal with. Apparently there are numerous species of grey mullet; those to be found in a fishmonger's are not, one hopes, the fish which the French call *cochons de mer* because they frequent harbours and muddy estuaries and feed off sewage outfalls and other nasties that find their way into the water.

The reputation of the grey mullet tends to suffer also from its name – it is not grey but silver, and has a sleek look about it. I bought one for the first time one weekend and baked it in foil, with some parsley, oil and white wine. The flesh is firm and in a blind tasting could easily be confused with bass or bream – yet it cost only a fraction over £2 a pound. The following day it tasted almost as good in a salad, with oil and lemon, capers and chopped chervil.

Then there is the grey mullet roe, variously known as *botargo*, *bottarga* and *boutargue*. Much of it comes from Sardinia, and especially from a fishing village on the south-west coast called Buggerru, where the roe is salted, cured and then sealed in wax. It goes well on a dry biscuit, but is more solid than smoked cod's roe, and may need some olive oil poured on it. The Italians sometimes grate their *bottarga* over pasta. However, if we are judging the insides of mullet, grey and red, I think I will go for the liver of the *rouget*.

Having already mentioned the red mullet's liver in the text, it is worth reiterating that a fishmonger who offers to clean the fish should always be asked to keep the liver for you. It is because of the quality of its liver that red mullet have sometimes been called sea woodcock.

Salmon

Salmo salar, the Atlantic salmon, is a most remarkable fish. Having gone to sea, where it has to run the gauntlet of modern deep-sea trawlers, it returns, a year or up to three years later, to the river of its birth to spawn. On the way it may fall prey to seals, to estuarial nets and to disease emanating from salmon farms. Once in the river it may have to leap up and over waterfalls (*salar* means the leaper) as it swims upstream, eating nothing until, having spawned, it dies in the river or returns to the sea. In this final phase of its life it is known as a kelt.

There has been a worrying dearth of wild Scottish salmon, although some improvement was seen in 2004 in the east coast rivers, following a reduction in drift netting offshore. The major problem, at least on the west coast of Scotland, has been attributable to salmon farms, which are liable to pollute the surrounding waters, with chemicals used to control parasites and disease, with waste and uneaten food. The wild stock may also be affected by disease spread by farmed fish which have escaped.

However, things are looking up. Some salmon farms have been forced out of business by competition from Norway, and an increasing number of farms now have their pens sited farther out to sea – particularly off the Orkneys and Shetlands – where the water is clean, currents will spread the wastes, the fish will be healthier and may not need to be given chemical additives. Such fish may be given the oxymoron description of 'farmed wild', or 'organic', a much-abused term which some suppliers insist allows them to add 'natural chemicals' to a fish's diet.

But the salmon may ingest harmful chemicals with their fishmeal diet. The fear is that much of the fish used to make meal contains dioxins from the highly toxic bed of the North Sea. One might suppose that at least wild salmon are free from nasty chemical infection. But I was told the other day by a fishmonger that some fish sold as wild in Europe will have come from the seas off the Russian coast which are far more polluted than the waters around salmon farms.

None of this makes shopping for salmon a simple exercise. Though farmed salmon is not as cheap as it was, the wild fish may still be up to five times more expensive – and it will be hard to convince oneself that it is five times better. The best bet may be to go for the fish that has been farmed in open, northerly waters and pay around £6 per pound for steaks or fillets. Some of the cheaper salmon will have an unpleasantly 'fishy' or oily smell and flavour, possibly due to an excess of sand-eel protein in its diet. (It is a mistake to imagine that salmon was always a luxury until the advent of farmed fish. In the eighteenth century it was often written into the contracts of servants and apprentices that they should not have to eat salmon more than twice a week.)

I know there are those – my wife was one – who hold that a salmon should only be cooked in one way: poached in a fish kettle, then eaten with new potatoes, sliced cucumber and a stiff mayonnaise. She would also insist, quite rightly, that salmon must be undercooked, most easily by bringing the water to the boil, simmering the fish gently for five minutes, then taking it off the heat and leaving it in the water for another 20 minutes.

Of the various ways of dealing with boned pieces of salmon, it is hard to beat the recipe famously invented by the Troisgros brothers at their three-starred restaurant in Roanne. The fish is briefly grilled and accompanied by a sorrel sauce, made by first reducing fish stock, wine and vermouth, then adding double cream, with a further reduction, chopped sorrel leaves and butter with the aid of a whisk. Salmon fish cakes are another near-classic, and best made without potato. The cooked and flaked fish should be combined with a white sauce, adding an egg yolk and chopped parsley or chives. Let the mixture cool before forming the cakes, coating them in breadcrumbs and frying them. The Russian fish pie known as *coulibiac* (variously spelt) is also a great favourite, but rather too time-consuming to make often at home. Salmon kedgeree is less successful, I find, than one made with smoked haddock.

I'm not sure I would always be able to tell the difference between wild and farmed salmon when smoked; the important thing is that the smoked fish should not be dry and it must be thinly sliced. It would be no hardship to me to eat a few slices of the best smoked salmon, with lemon juice and black pepper, every day for the rest of my life. While this remains an idle dream, I may instead celebrate this midsummer season with the pale and delectable flesh of the wild salmon, and Foremost new potatoes cooked with fresh mint.

Depending on the conditions in which they are kept and the composition of their diet, there need be nothing wrong with farmed salmon. The wild fish should be given a break, and time to recover their stocks.

Crab

It was Celia Johnson, when she was able to get away from the West End theatre and walk along the north Cornish coast, who taught me how to catch crabs. Using a pole with a hooked and pointed metal end, not unlike a shortened shepherd's crook, you probe the fissures in rocks which emerge at very low tides and hope to bring out a large brown crab, with a fat, fearsome claw gripping the hook. This, at any rate, is the method recommended to young amateur fishermen who will flock to the beaches of Devon and Cornwall for their school holidays. The narrow holes in the rocks often go back a long way and, with a bit of experience, you quickly learn to distinguish between the noise of the hook striking rock and the more hollow tap as it makes contact with a crab's back shell. Then comes the excitement of trying to coax and pull the crab out of its hole and into a bag or bucket.

There are plenty of other, smaller crabs which may be encountered in rock pools or in the shallows: some black-shelled, which nip ferociously, and feeler crabs which can be used as bait for bass. But the brown crab is just about the only one eaten in this country. (Spider crabs, of which more in a minute, used to be thrown back when they were caught here. Now they are sent off to France or Spain, where they are properly appreciated.)

I once asked a fishmonger on the Norfolk-Suffolk border if he could sell me some crab claws, as I didn't much like the brown meat, only to be asked rather sniffily if I had ever eaten a Cromer crab, whose brown meat was quite different from the inferior crabs of the West Country. But it has never tasted very different to me, and always reminds me of the Shippam's pastes of my youth.

Rather than eat a dressed crab from the shell, I prefer to separate the brown meat and mix it in a blender with mayonnaise, Worcestershire sauce, Tabasco and lemon juice, then spoon it over some lettuce leaves and add the white meat. Crab claws are widely available nowadays – I have heard that one claw is sometimes removed from a live crab before it is returned to the sea for the claw to grow again – and their white flesh is, to my mind, almost as good as a lobster's. It may be sprinkled with paprika and eaten with samphire, devilled with Dijon mustard, cream and brandy, made into rissoles with a cheese sauce, made into cakes with mayonnaise, breadcrumbs, beaten egg and mustard powder, or mixed with scrambled eggs. It makes a good pasty, though not often found in Cornwall, and in Donegal a crab pie is made with chopped celery, parsley, cider and nutmeg.

Crab – blue, soft-shelled and, best of all, Alaskan king – is hugely popular in the United States, but is outside the scope of this book. The smaller crabs of the Mediterranean are to be seen in most coastal fish markets and tend to go into fish soups. And then there is the spider crab, with a pear-shaped, spiky shell and spidery legs, but no real claws. It is much in demand in France and Spain, yet largely ignored in this country, although there are plenty of them to be found in our waters. Unless you make a special request, before they are all whisked off to the continent, you will be lucky to find a spider crab at an English fishmonger's.

In some Spanish supermarkets you can buy a live spider crab (*centolla*) and have it boiled on the premises (about 10 minutes per pound) while you finish your shopping. If you can find one here – preferably a female which is carrying its eggs – take the meat and coral from the shell and legs and enjoy the deliciously sweet flesh. But it may be simpler to wait until the next trip to Spain, or to Brittany or to the South of France where spider crabs are called *araignées*.

In the Basque country a dish called *txangurro* should not be missed. The spider crab's meat is combined with sautéed onion, garlic and carrot, also chopped tomatoes, fish stock, white wine and paprika, then placed in the crab's shell and baked with a topping of breadcrumbs and parsley. It's a pity about the spider crab having no fat claws, but its body meat is better than that of any crab from Cromer.

Cock crabs have larger claws and, therefore, more white meat. They can be identified by their tail-flap, which is smaller than the female's.

Whiting

Whiting does not seem to be fashionable these days – perhaps it never was – but in my early twentieth-century edition of the *Encyclopaedia Britannica* it is described as 'one of the most valuable food fishes of northern Europe'. This may be due in part to its not necessarily enviable reputation as being good for invalids. It is said to be wholesome and digestible, especially when steamed, but unfortunately the 'invalid' tag puts one in mind of hospitals and old people's homes where the smell from the kitchen of watery, overcooked cabbage mingles with the smell of watery, overcooked and not entirely fresh fish. Whiting deserves better than that.

Its range stretches from Iceland to the Mediterranean; it is often taken in shallow water, close inshore, yet it is possibly the least-known member of the cod family. Haddock, hake, coley, pollack are all more often found at the fishmonger's. Indeed, so rarely is the whiting sighted in Wiltshire that I had some trouble getting it. Apparently it is considered, by fishmongers at least, to be inferior to haddock and hake, and its price has been forced up by the demand for whiting from France and Spain. But I was able to buy whiting fillets at £5.50 per pound, delivered to my door from Cornwall for a small charge, and the service was so quick and efficient, also including a free kilo of smoked salmon for new customers, that the company responsible, Fishworks, deserves a plug.

For some unaccountable reason, whiting used to be served whole with the tail twisted around and put in the mouth of the fish, which is described as *en colère*. (Anyone would be pretty angry to have their tail stuffed into their mouth. The whiting in *Alice's Adventures in Wonderland* wasn't very pleased, as he said to the slow-moving snail, to have his tail trodden on by a porpoise.) When the fish is cooked whole, it is usually split down the back, rather than the stomach, to remove the backbone; however, my experience with whiting is confined to the fillets, with not a tail in sight.

A whiting dinner was prepared last month in Wiltshire. First, a Spanish soup, *caldo gaditano* (of Cadiz), incorporating olive oil, garlic cloves (later discarded), chopped onion, fish stock, parsley and pieces of whiting. After 10 minutes of simmering, orange and lemon juice were added. (The recipe said Seville oranges, but where do you get them in midsummer?) For the next dish, *merlans à la verdurette*, the whiting fillets were coated in egg and breadcrumbs and fried, then sprinkled with chopped shallots, mushrooms (using what I think were small chanterelles), parsley, chives and tarragon, which had all been fried in butter.

Both this and the third offering, *merlans à l'orange*, come from Jane Grigson's *Fish Cookery*. Again the fillets are fried and a sauce is made with double cream, egg yolks, white wine, black and cayenne pepper and the juice of Seville oranges, or sweet orange mixed with lemon. The tasting panel judged the whiting to be beautifully fresh, with good flakes, and a clean, mild flavour. The orange and lemon combination with the fish was thought to be a great success in the soup, and would have been even better with the fillets had they been poached or baked. The *merlans à la verdurette* were widely praised.

I had never come across fish with orange before, but it worked surprisingly well, with the juice of one lemon added to two sweet oranges. And I was intrigued to learn that Jane Grigson's recipe, using Seville oranges, came originally from

an English eighteenth-century cookery book. Who knows
how long it has been popular in south-west Spain?

Another sauce which goes well with whiting is made with
samphire; it should be ready for picking now on the
Norfolk coast and is often to be found at a fishmonger's.
Boiled and then puréed with butter, it is deliciously salty
and bright green. Although whiting may sometimes be hard
to find in this country, there is no such problem in France.
For those who are about to spend summer holidays there,
merlan is generally available in the markets and may cost as
little as €7 per kilo. Other members of the cod family,
whose French names may be unfamiliar, will also be on
sale, usually filleted: *lingue* or *julienne* (ling), *lieu noir*
(coley or saithe), *lieu jaune* (pollack). My advice, however,
is to go for *merlan*, and forget about the invalids.

*Some fishmongers don't bother with this
underrated fish, judging that there is little demand
for it. But it is well worth seeking out, when absolutely
fresh. When the flesh turns soft, don't buy it.*

Lobster

Do we keep enough British lobsters for ourselves? I was pondering this question a while ago as I watched a container lorry leaving the Hebridean island of Tiree which would deliver its load of live lobsters four days later to the fish market in Madrid. The demand for lobsters in Spain and France seems almost limitless, but I wonder if we don't suffer by having to pay a higher price for the number left for the British market, or by being fobbed off with lobsters from the other side of the Atlantic. (The lobsters at Waitrose come from Nova Scotia, for heaven's sake.) At least we don't have to eat those inferior lobsters from the warm waters of the Caribbean or the Indian Ocean.

In winter there may be a shortage here, due to the fact that some fishermen keep their pots out of the water for several months; but in summer, at least, the native lobsters seem to be plentiful. A National Lobster Hatchery has recently begun breeding them in tanks and feeding them on plankton. At around three months, divers take them to the seabed where they are released. This sounds an excellent idea, but I doubt if it will result in the price of lobster being any less than the £10-£14 per pound being charged this year.

They may be a bit cheaper bought live, which I prefer. Not only do you avoid the risk of them being overcooked and not entirely fresh, but you may also wish to grill rather than boil them. The question then arises of how best to dispatch the unfortunate crustacean. The RSPCA used to insist that it was cruel to plunge a lobster into boiling water, because it could take more than a minute to die, and that the kinder way was to immerse it in cold water which would then be brought gradually to boiling-point. Predictably, the RSPCA was shown to be wrong about this, and anyway, the slow cooking process has the effect of drawing out and losing the lobster's juices. Accepted opinion now is that quick boiling is the most humane method; if the lobster is to be split when alive, it should first be sent to sleep for about 45 minutes in a deep freeze.

It is a great mistake to boil a lobster for too long. Twelve minutes is usually enough (in sea water or salted water), so that when the claws are cracked a milky liquid will ooze out. And if the coral has not quite turned from black to red, it will still taste delicious. If the live but anaesthetised lobster is cut in half, it should be grilled on a high heat for about eight minutes with melted butter poured over the flesh. After cooking, a sauce consisting of butter, fish stock, lemon juice and chopped herbs (including tarragon or basil) might be added.

Lobster is such a treat that you tend to remember where and how you ate it. I recall spending a few days in Maine where lobster meat is bought and bagged in the local store, rather as if one were buying sausages from a butcher. In some Chinese restaurants you may be presented with a live lobster which then reappears on a plate cooked with ginger and spring onions. Most memorably, I had, as a starter in a Paris restaurant last year, a scrambled goose's egg mixed with pieces of lobster, put back into the egg's shell and served with buttered toast 'soldiers'.

A cold lobster with properly made mayonnaise, spiked perhaps with a little mustard powder, and a few lettuce leaves is hard to beat. So too is fresh lobster bisque, although a bit of a performance to make oneself. I have been looking again at *Madame Prunier's Fish Cookery Book*, published in the 1930s, which has pages of lobster dishes, most of them with heart-stoppingly rich sauces involving truffles, cream, egg yolks and brandy. Lobster

Thermidor and Newburg are two that I remember were popular some years ago. One simpler recipe, *homard à la Bretonne*, I followed successfully with the lobster which my Tiree hosts kindly gave me to take home. The pieces of lobster, together with any coral and the green liver, are mixed with prawns and chopped mushrooms and added to a cream and white wine sauce flavoured with onion. It goes well with rice, and can be prettified by returning the mixture to the shells, sprinkling with grated cheese and browning briefly under the grill.

Ideally, pick a lobster of no more than one kilo in weight, and if buying it cooked, try to ensure that it has not been boiled for more than 15 minutes.

Grouse / Partridge

The red grouse is a resilient little bird. Prone to an unpleasant disease called louping ill which is transmitted by sheep ticks, and vulnerable to attack by nasty, invasive little worms, its population may crash in some moorland areas for several years; and then it will reappear in healthy numbers as if nothing had happened. I have only recently learnt that the Dr Edward Wilson who did so much valuable work in the early-twentieth century on the causes of grouse disease is the same Wilson who perished with Scott in the Antarctic.

In these days, when field sports seem to be constantly under threat from interfering ignoramuses, it is heartening to know, from a report by the Game Conservancy Trust, that the management of grouse moors benefits birds such as the curlew, dunlin and golden plover, whereas in upland areas where there is no grouse shooting, the numbers of those birds are in decline. The evidence is directly contrary to a statement issued from that deeply discredited organisation, the RSPB, that 'where wild birds and animals are in decline the hand of man... can be detected'.

Grouse moor management, however, does come at a cost – something like £150 per brace for the privilege of shooting them as they hurtle towards your butt. So rare are the occasions when I have been invited to shoot grouse that I am pretty inexpert both at killing and at cooking them other than by plain roasting – which, with most game, is usually the best way. Whether the bird comes to you straight from the moor or from a butcher, oven-ready, try to ensure that it is a young one. There is absolutely no point in paying an exorbitant sum of money to a restaurant to eat grouse on the 12th, since it should be hung for about four days before being plucked and drawn.

The grouse should be smeared with butter, bacon rashers placed over the breasts, roasted in a hot oven for about 15 minutes, with frequent basting, and then left to rest. Plenty of bread sauce will be required, also white breadcrumbs fried in butter and then added to the bacon, finely chopped. The bird should be placed on a piece of fried bread spread with its liver, which will have been gently cooked in butter and brandy. Little more is needed, except perhaps watercress or boiled cabbage, a thin gravy and some rowanberry jelly.

Most recipe books distinguish between young and old grouse, the latter more suitable for casseroling, making a pie or a terrine. If roasting a bird of indeterminate age, it can be cooked slowly in the oven, in a little water and covered with tinfoil, for 45 minutes before discarding water and foil and roasting it on a high heat for another 10 minutes. With the luxury of several birds, an old-fashioned cold grouse salad would make a tempting picnic, possibly with sliced beetroot and hard-boiled egg and a herby, creamy mustard dressing.

Next season, one always hopes, the grouse will avoid disease and bad weather, and then – who knows? – this king of game birds may be a little less expensive in the shops.

Partridge, in season from next month, is preferred to grouse and pheasant by many people, but I find the flesh of the red-legged or French bird (the one most commonly seen and sold) rather bland. When my uncle, August Courtauld, spent the winter of 1930-31 alone on the Greenland icecap, he recorded in his diary his longing to get back home to huge breakfasts of poached eggs, kidneys and cold partridge. I am sure he was thinking of the tastier, gamier grey or English partridge, which was much more plentiful in those days. Now, when restaurants and butchers offer grey partridges, the chances are they will be farmed birds which have never flown over a line of guns.

The French partridge, in my view, needs more flavours than a conventional roasting can provide. In France it is often casseroled, with cabbage, bacon and smoked sausage, carrots, grated lemon peel and nutmeg. A German method uses sauerkraut, juniper berries, white wine and sour cream. In Spain (where large numbers of these partridges are shot), the bird may be cooked with garlic, onion, thyme and oloroso sherry, or fried in oil, then simmered in dry sherry, stock and Seville oranges with pieces of serrano ham. When the liquid has been reduced, and the oranges mashed and pressed through a sieve, they will make a thick, marmalade-like sauce.

For those who insist on straightforward roasting, with gravy and bread sauce, make sure the partridge has been well hung and surround it with a variety of wild autumn mushrooms.

Pointed primary feathers indicate a young bird; if the toenails are falling out, it is too old for roasting. If you can wait for grouse until late in the season (after mid-October), they should be less expensive to buy.

Herring

'Jack likes a herring for his tea,' I remember, years ago, our gardener's wife used to say. That was before herring stocks crashed in the 1970s and the fishery was closed for several years. Herring gradually returned to the North Sea, but a lot of people, like Jack, had by then found something else to satisfy their appetites after work. It may be hard for many of us to remember how popular this fish used to be. Fifty years ago, there were books devoted to the herring, and in Jane Grigson's invaluable work, *Fish Cookery*, first published in 1973, herring recipes take up a page of the index.

In past centuries the economic health of many northern European maritime towns was entirely dependent on the herring. Yarmouth's grant of borough status in 1108 came with an obligation to pay the monarch 'ten milliard of herrings' a year, and for centuries it held an annual herring fair which could last for several weeks. The decline of the Hanseatic towns of the Baltic coast was largely attributable to the movement of the huge shoals of herring into the North Sea. Then it was the turn of the Dutch and Norwegians to develop their own herring industry.

There is plenty of herring about today, but it doesn't feature much in modern cookery books, and most of the British catch is exported – to Russia, Africa and the Far East. The point is worth making – at least as a corrective to Charles 'Jeremiah' Clover's recent book on overfishing and endangered fish stocks – that herring numbers are now so healthy that the quota may be increased again.

This is the middle of the Scottish herring season, and reports from Peterhead indicate that the fish are of good size and quality. What could be nicer than a lightly grilled herring, at any time of day, with a slice or two of brown bread? The best way of dealing with all those tiresome bones is to cut along the belly of the fish before cooking, then flatten it, skin side up, and press down firmly on the backbone. It will then be simpler to remove, together with at least some of the smaller bones.

The Scots way with herrings is to cover them with oatmeal and fry them in bacon fat, possibly adding a cream and mustard sauce at the end. They may also be rubbed before cooking with mustard powder or made mustard and sprinkled with breadcrumbs, then basted with melted butter. Some recipes advise making a sauce with the herring's soft roes. This I have not tried, but the roes are delicious on their own, poached, fried or grilled. Chopped parsley and cream may be added, but the important thing is to eat them on hot buttered toast with a good shake of the Worcestershire sauce bottle.

Fresh herring is not widely eaten in Scandinavia, where the preferred method is to salt or pickle the fish. Large quantities of marinated herring are exported to this country, in addition to the ever-popular 'rollmops' prepared in Scotland. Of course it is perfectly possible to salt the herrings yourself, but the so-called *matjes* fillets are readily available, requiring only the addition of sliced cooking apple, soured cream, chopped onion and paprika for an excellent first course. Alternatively, use fresh cream with mustard or horseradish, and mix with some salad potatoes and chopped chives.

And what about the kipper, that wonderful Northumbrian invention of the mid-nineteenth century? It is the mildest of all cured herrings (the strongest was the 'red herring', which used to be sent out to the slave plantations of the West Indies and the American South) and, if the fish is fat, has been briefly brined and smoked and not dyed, it fully deserves its reputation. Whether the taste of a kipper is more likely to stay with you for hours if you have grilled rather than boiled it, I am uncertain. But I do know that kippers are better digested if taken with a glass of Champagne or black velvet.

Buckling is hot-smoked and in my experience rather disappointing, but bloaters – which some readers may be unaware of, unless they live in East Anglia – should not be missed. Smoked whole, with the guts left in, they have an attractively gamey flavour when grilled. An old Norfolk recipe recommends mixing the flesh with scrambled eggs; and I have also just come across the idea of filling an omelette with soft herring roes cooked in butter. Intriguing new combinations to try.

When we are being urged to eat fish with sustainable stocks, the herring should come high on the list – and it is an oily fish rich in Omega 3.

Perch

I have recently acquired a charming little book by Ambrose Heath called *From Creel to Kitchen*. Published in 1939, it offers recipes for 20 species of freshwater fish caught in our rivers and lakes, including carp, char, grayling, barbel, chub, gudgeon, roach and tench. It had not occurred to me that there are apparently more species of fish in fresh water than in the sea, although I doubt many readers would be impressed by my devoting much time to dace or rudd. But I do think perch deserves more than a passing mention.

Izaak Walton, who was knowledgeable on the subject of eating as well as catching fish, and who is much quoted in Heath's book, wrote of the perch that the Germans considered it to be 'so wholesome that physicians allow him to be eaten by wounded men, or by men in fevers, or by women in childbed'. Madame Prunier called it 'a beautiful and excellent fish', and others consider it, after salmon and trout, to be the most delicate of the river fish.

Heath suggests a number of recipes for perch: fried, grilled, baked with a hollandaise sauce, or stewed in stock and sherry, together with garlic, parsley, nutmeg and anchovy sauce. Jane Grigson, who also rates perch highly, has a regional Italian recipe. The perch fillets are marinated in olive oil and lemon juice, with chopped spring onions, then dipped in flour, egg and breadcrumbs and fried in butter and oil. Chopped sage and butter are poured over the fish at the last minute. From France comes a recipe which requires the whole fish, slit with a knife on each side, to be put in a casserole on a bed of sliced onion and celeriac cut into julienne strips. This is simmered in white wine for 10 minutes, with cloves and seeded chilli peppers which are then discarded. Having reduced the cooking liquid, a sauce is made with a *beurre manié*, whisking it into the wine reduction with more butter and chopped parsley.

There is one problem here: perch are not easy to find in this country, unless you catch them yourself (in which case beware of the dorsal fins, which have very painful, even poisonous, spikes). They are more readily available in

France and Holland, where there are generally two other options: a related fish known in English as pike-perch, and the imported Nile perch. (Lake Geneva, if you happen to live nearby, is full of perch.)

The *perche du Nil*, which can be bought, filleted, all over France, is said to come from Lake Victoria, where the White Nile has its source. It is also caught by game fishermen in Lake Nasser, on the Egypt-Sudan border and can reach over 200 pounds. With a gentle flavour and good texture, it is suitable for baking in foil, which was the way a friend and I cooked it last month in France, adding a few queen scallops briefly fried with shallots and garlic and mixed with a tin of *petits pois* and lettuce. Warm applause from our hosts, who thought it was sea bass.

The pike-perch, which is sometimes called zander, is common in France where its name is *sandre*. According to a useful booklet issued by the Fishmongers' Company, it was introduced into British lakes and rivers in the last century, but was apparently so successful in wiping out other wildlife in the water that it has been heavily culled, although not to extinction. (Why did we never get to eat all the pike-perch that were killed?) In France, this fish appears to co-exist happily enough with other species in rivers such as the Loire and Rhône, and it is quite delicious. Its flavour has been compared to a sole; I have enjoyed it baked with a red wine sauce (one of the best fish dishes I have had this year), also grilled with lemon juice, and I saw it offered on a menu in Provence *au beurre basilic*.

The French appreciate fish which live in what they call *eau douce*, but we do not, restricting ourselves to the questionable pleasure of eating farmed rainbow trout – not to be confused with those delectable little brown trout caught in upland lakes and rivers. Zander, pike and carp are considered here as sport fish, which are fit for anglers but not for the table. (We may be right about carp, which in my experience is a disappointing fish best left to central Europeans who apparently enjoy eating it on Christmas Eve.) Nile perch are equally neglected in this country, although sold almost everywhere else in Europe. English perch were popular a few hundred years ago, especially in Tudor times, and Ambrose Heath includes a recipe for the fish 'Hampton Court fashion'. It is time the fashion was revived.

They may be hard to find in this country, with fishmongers insisting there is no demand. Tell the fishmonger that you are creating a demand.

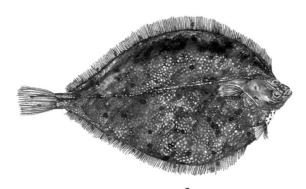

Plaice

Y ou don't want to eat plaice, they say in East Anglia, until the corn is in the ear. Others don't want to eat plaice at all, judging it to be a little below the salt. Larousse comments patronisingly, with the faintest of praise, that 'this fish, though of medium quality, is quite good, provided it is perfectly fresh'. Madame Prunier is more damning, saying of plaice that 'it is not a prime fish, and is not used at all in high cookery'. Constance Spry writes dismissively: 'It is one of the duller fish and relies on accompaniments for flavour'. I must protest: when beautifully fresh, and at this time of year, when the fillets are fat and glistening, plaice is one of the best, and incidentally the whitest, of white fish.

The French, for some reason, have two different words for plaice (*carrelet* and *plie*), but they don't really rate it.

And since it is not a Mediterranean fish, you won't find it in Italy, and I have never seen it in a market or on a menu in Spain. Plaice is a fish of the North Sea, the Irish Sea, the English Channel, and most of our EU fishing 'partners' are not interested. Which is not to say that this fish is unknown in French cooking; it was for plaice that Monsieur Dugléré was said to have invented the sauce that bears his name. But he may have thought that such a dull fish needed the addition of onions, tomatoes, herbs, garlic and white wine in order to make it palatable.

The point can bear repetition: if plaice is not fresh, if the fillets have a dull appearance and have begun to turn slightly grey or yellow, like a used flannel, don't buy them. They won't be worth cooking, even in M Dugléré's way. At its best, plaice should be filleted, skinned and fried, having been coated in flour or egg and breadcrumbs, and eaten with nothing more than mashed potato, a sprinkling of lemon juice and possibly tartare sauce. (My wife disagreed, insisting on baking her plaice in cream, and eating it with toast and butter, which may have had something to do with her Suffolk childhood.) If you have access to a deep fryer and very hot oil, then the plaice fillets may be battered (with self-raising flour and beer or soda water), ensuring that the fish remains perfectly – I wish I could find another word – moist. Plaice may also be successfully grilled on the bone (the skins should be removed after cooking) and eaten with browned butter.

Although I am not normally a fan of fish with cheese, there are some appealing recipes which involve baking plaice fillets with onion, mushrooms and grated cheese. I have also heard of plaice combined with Jerusalem artichokes. But the accompaniments should never overwhelm the fish which, *pace* Spry, does have a most delicate flavour and texture.

We cannot, however, claim plaice as an exclusively British fish. It is, after, all caught in the North Sea, and the Baltic, and is popular in Germany and Scandinavia. I am grateful to Alan Davidson's excellent book, *North Atlantic Seafood*, for the information that in Denmark plaice is fried with bacon, and also eaten with cranberry sauce – a combination I am prepared to leave to the Danes.

Plaice are, or were, frequently on the menu at the outstanding Irish hotel, Ballymaloe House in County Cork. I remember them being quite small, but since they were caught from a trawler in Ballycotton Bay, they could not have been fresher. Little plaice should not be confused with the similar-looking flounder and dab, which are better known in Cockney rhyming slang than they are as fish for the table. Large plaice can grow to three pounds or more and live for up to 30 years, and it is, as I say, when they are fat that they are so delectable.

For anyone living within half an hour's drive of Hungerford, I can strongly recommend a visit on a Friday morning, when a fishmonger from Hull parks his van in the High Street and, throughout the summer and at least until the end of the year, sells quantities of large, fresh plaice fillets, at the unbeatable price of £3.90 per pound. They may come from not far offshore in the North Sea, or from as far as the waters round Iceland, but they are always, as he rightly describes them, superb. These are decidedly not lower-class fish.

Spawning takes place in early spring, when plaice should be avoided. The large, fat specimens come into their own in the second half of the year.

Duck/Goose

In the past I have kept Indian Runner ducks – with their long necks and shuffling gait they provide much amusement for children – Khaki Campbells for their egg-laying, and Muscovy ducks, which have intelligence and character. But I never ate any of them. It was not until later that I learnt that Muscovy ducks, also known as Barbary ducks, have a higher proportion of lean breast meat than other ducks, and that in France they are crossed with Pekin and Rouen ducks to produce foie gras. But our Muscovy ducks, which would wag their tail feathers when they were about to be fed, were really farm pets.

A recent crossbreed, mating mallard with Pekin, has produced a duck reared in Suffolk and sold as Gressingham, which also has plenty of breast meat (*magret* in French). Apparently all domestic ducks, except for the Muscovy which originally came from South America, were bred from the mallard – including the Aylesbury and Norfolk strains, which are probably what we get when we buy a duck for roasting.

To ensure that it has a crispy skin when cooked, prick the duck all over with a fork, pour boiling water over it and repeat the exercise, then leave the bird to cool for an hour or so (the Chinese hang their ducks out to dry) before roasting it in a hot oven for at least an hour. I find it hard to resist a sage and onion stuffing with duck (the invention of a famous philandering naval captain, Sir Kenelm Digby, in the seventeenth century), also a strong gravy.

Distant memories of *duck à l'orange*, in the days when every nice young girl trained at the Cordon Bleu cookery school in London was liable to smother a duck with not only a thick orange gravy, but also honey and cherries as well, have rather put me off these sweet combinations. But I have nothing against a *sauce bigarade*, made with bitter Seville oranges (juice and zest), plus stock, the duck juices, a little sugar and a glass of Madeira. While apple sauce is traditionally offered with duck, the Welsh prefer theirs with onion sauce. Peas are a classic accompanying vegetable; so too are turnips which, when roasted round the bird, will absorb some of its fat.

Although a domestic duck should always be well cooked, the breasts, which are often sold separately, are better served pinkish – whether or not they are then thinly sliced and arranged poncily on the plate in the shape of a fan. They could then be eaten with mashed potato and a simple sauce made with soy, red wine, chopped shallots and a spoonful of raspberry vinegar. Slightly qualifying what I have said about duck and fruit flavours, a sauce made with *membrillo* (Spanish quince paste) and sherry goes well with any duck, farmed or wild. So does the fruit of sloes, which have been soaked in gin, stuffed into the cavity of the bird, then pressed through a sieve after cooking and added to stock made from the giblets and wine vinegar.

Wild duck, coming into season this month, should definitely be eaten quite rare; and a roast mallard is more easily carved if the breast meat is first removed from the bone and then sliced. My favourite is teal, very tricky to shoot as they flash past in the gathering dusk before coming to rest on the water, and wonderful to eat (two per person is not unreasonable). With roast teal (15 minutes in a hot oven) Rowley Leigh does a wine and shallot sauce, thickened with a *beurre manié* and poured over the birds with a good helping of bubble and squeak.

Wild geese, which it is illegal to sell and are only, in effect, available to those who shoot them, are not worth eating anyway, unless the bird is young and is barded and basted during cooking to stop it drying out. A domestic goose, on the other hand, is full of fat and the time of year for enjoying it is approaching. For those who are reluctant to wait until Christmas, the festival of St Michael, on 29 September, used to mark the end of harvest and the date on which farms changed hands and debts and rents were paid, celebrated by the roasting of the Michaelmas goose.

With plenty of windfall apples around later this month, it would be wasteful not to use some to make a sauce or to stuff the bird, together perhaps with sage, onion, sausagemeat, breadcrumbs and port. Prunes, apricots and seasonal walnuts are also used as stuffing for goose, which should be given 20 minutes per pound in a medium oven. The potatoes will, of course, be roasted in goose fat, and the remainder kept for cooking all sorts of other things (see Jeanne Strang's *Goose Fat and Garlic*).

There are those, notably Elizabeth David and Jane Grigson, who prefer to eat goose cold. So did Sir Kenelm Digby, pickling his in salt, vinegar, wine, ginger and cloves.

As a fatty bird, duck is best bought fresh; if it is frozen for more than a couple of months it will begin to deteriorate. Allow one and a half pounds' weight per person.

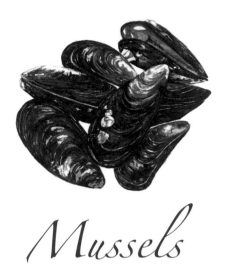

Mussels

I am ashamed to recall that, 10 or so years ago, to accompany an article written for *Harpers & Queen* on, I think, some of the food to be found on the coasts of Britain, I was persuaded to allow myself to be photographed with shirtsleeve rolled up and a mussel balanced on my forearm. 'Mussel man', or something equally embarrassing, was the headline given to the piece; and the ribald comments I received were all deserved.

It wasn't even a British mussel, but one of those large bivalves from New Zealand which are sometimes unappealingly described in supermarkets as 'green-lipped'. Home-grown mussels, gathered oneself from rocks which are submerged at high tide, are no less tasty for being smaller. Larger ones, which can be found at the mouths of estuaries and in harbours where sewage may be responsible for their size, should probably be avoided, but these days, farmed mussels of an equivalent size are grown off the west coast of Scotland on ropes suspended from floating platforms.

Popular as they are in Britain, and in Ireland, one thinks first of France or Belgium as the home of mussels, and of that ubiquitous, wonderfully cheap, and much advertised dish of *moules frites* (which does not, as I once thought, mean fried mussels). I well remember eating bowls of them one evening, sitting at a table in the *vieux port* of La Rochelle and watching the sun go down behind the twin towers at the harbour entrance.

Almost any dish has to start with the steaming of the mussels, in a little white wine or cider, with chopped shallot and parsley. One is told not to use any mussels whose shells are open before they are cooked, but they need not be discarded until they have first been tapped sharply on a hard surface. If the mussel is alive, it will close its shells and is quite safe to use. Apart from the traditional way with mussels *à la mariniere*, there are *moules à la crème*, *niçoise* (with a pestou sauce), *bordelaise* (with tomato, garlic and breadcrumbs), *ariegeoise* (with pieces of sausage and ham, which I had last month south of Toulouse) and, a favourite of mine, *mouclade*.

I was shown how to do this dish a couple of years ago at Rick Stein's Padstow Seafood School. The liquor from the cooked mussels (minus the last spoonful or two, which may be sandy) should be stirred into a sauce consisting of melted butter, chopped garlic, curry powder, a little flour, brandy and saffron. When this is simmering, add crème fraîche, reduce the sauce slightly and pour it over the mussels.

At the cookery school you may also do a clam chowder, which works equally well with mussels. Chopped bacon and onion are gently fried, then added to a saucepan of milk, cream, diced potatoes, bay leaf and mussel liquor and boiled for about five minutes. Add the chopped mussels and parsley at the last minute. A mussel soup can be made by playing around with any of these ingredients in various combinations. If you put together the onion, garlic, saffron, cream and parsley, with some sliced tomatoes and leeks and a little rice, you have the *potage Billy-By* originally created by Maxim's in Paris.

When I have gathered mussels myself, I sometimes remove them from their shells after steaming, then immerse them in olive oil and lemon juice, to be eaten cold as a snack with French bread. Mussels also go well with spinach, and in an omelette, if they are small. Which reminds me to mention Elizabeth David's delicious recipe for *les oeufs du pêcheur*, apparently invented by a French dressmaker. Poached eggs are placed on pieces of fried bread in ramekin dishes, covered with hot cream and grated cheese briefly melted in the oven. The relevance of the *pêcheur* is that the eggs are poached in the liquor obtained from cooking a few pints of mussels.

A couple of years ago, I went to what is probably the mussel capital of Europe – Vigo, in northern Spain, where hundreds of thousands of rope-grown mussels supply more than 50 per cent of the total European market. Vigo is also Spain's principal fishing port and I was invited to its World Fishing Exhibition, where I well remember working my way through a huge dish of mussels (*mejillones* in Spanish) and several other less familiar, but no less delicious, members of the bivalve family.

When not gathering mussels oneself from the rocks, those grown on ropes suspended beneath large floating platforms have the advantage of being generally clean, and of a good size and flavour.

Oysters

At the beginning of this month, after two weeks in south-west France (where I came across several fish unknown in this country), it was good to get back in time for the seafood festival on Mersea Island, in Essex, where we enjoyed the first Colchester native oysters of the season. A few more slipped delectably down with our seafood platter at the nearby Company Shed – bring your own wine, bread, mayonnaise – which was still doing good business well after four o'clock on a glorious afternoon.

This so-called European oyster, cultivated in England mainly in Essex, Suffolk, Kent and Cornwall, is sold only between September and April; in summer the roe may give it a milky appearance and a rather dull taste. It is rarer than, and more than twice the price of, the Pacific or

Portuguese all-year-round oyster, which grows to maturity more quickly and is widely available. In France these oysters have various names, depending where they have been gathered: *belons* and *armoricaines* from Brittany, *fines de claire* usually from the Charente further south. I was interested to see oysters from Oléron being sold in a market in the Lot – interested because my family lived on the Ile d'Oléron, off La Rochelle, until expelled, along with all Huguenots, by Louis XIV towards the end of the seventeenth century. (Oléron is known not only for the number and quality of the oyster beds which surround the island, but also for the fact that it was the last place in France to be liberated in 1945.)

How to describe the pleasure of eating a raw oyster? Spoilsports might wish to mention that you are eating the intestine, liver, gills and stomach of a hermaphrodite, but that is quite irrelevant to the lotus-oyster-eater. Eleanor Clark, in her classic, almost poetic book, *The Oysters of Locmariaquer* (on the southern Brittany coast), mentions 'that little stimulus on the palate' provided by an oyster. 'You are eating the sea, only the sensation of a gulp of sea water has been wafted out of it by some sorcery.'

The 'true oyster moment', as it has been called, can only be properly experienced by tipping the contents of the half-shell into your mouth – without a fork, without

Tabasco sauce or vinegar, and even, if it is a native oyster, without any lemon juice or pepper. No one would seriously argue – would they? – that there is a better way of eating oysters; but some people are in the habit of doing strange things with them. I cannot see the point of adding oysters to steak and kidney pudding, or of wrapping them in bacon and calling them Angels-on-Horseback. (A prune wrapped in bacon makes a much more satisfactory savoury.) A French recipe recommends eating a fried chipolata sausage immediately followed by an oyster, then repeating the questionable exercise 12 times. Why, I simply cannot imagine.

If you must cook oysters, use the foreign ones. Several recipes involve grilling or baking them, with grated cheese, which does not appeal to me, although I should say that I have never tried the combination. But I do remember enjoying oysters Rockefeller in the city, New Orleans, where the dish was invented. Chopped spinach, parsley, spring onion and crispy bacon are combined with breadcrumbs, salt and paprika and cooked in butter. The mixture is then placed on the opened oysters, browned briefly under a grill and moistened with a little Pernod. Unfortunately, the Americans do have other ways with oysters, which may involve smothering them with tomato ketchup or cooking them with cream and curry powder.

I have just tried a few of the cheaper oysters briefly poached, with spinach and *beurre blanc* – not bad at all – and I quite like the idea of oysters fried in tempura batter with a mayonnaise containing wasabi (Japanese green horseradish).

But let's get back to the joys of eating raw oysters. There is not much point in thinking longingly back to those Dickensian days when 200 oysters could be bought in London for four shillings and Sam Weller made his remark about poverty and oysters, commenting that 'the poorer the place is, the greater call there seems to be for oysters... here's a oyster stall to every half-dozen houses'. One should, however, allow oneself an occasional oyster blow-out. I recall a three-hour drive westwards across Ireland, one day in late April, to Moran's pub to catch the last of its famously good oysters before the season closed. They were still being served, and we were still relishing those oyster moments, with the assistance of pints of Guinness, as the light began to fade over Galway Bay.

When opening an oyster, hold it, flat side upwards, in your left hand wrapped in a cloth, then insert a wide-bladed kitchen knife (or, if you have one, an oyster-opening knife) into the hinge between the two shells and force them apart by agitating the knife.

Shark

The first barracuda to be caught in British waters was landed at Newlyn, Cornwall, five years ago. Giant fin whales were spotted in 2005 off the Pembrokeshire coast. The evidence of these alien visitors may be attributable to global warming, or to changes in the flow of ocean currents, but it makes one wonder if it may be only a matter of time before a fearsome great white shark moves up the Atlantic from its present killing grounds on the South African coast to the bathing beaches of north Cornwall (from where, watching a school of porpoises not being chased by a shark, I am writing).

I have fished for blue shark off this coast, and I remember once seeing a huge basking shark close to the boat from which we were fishing for mackerel. (Basking sharks are quite harmless, except if they happen to surface beneath your boat, which may be a good deal smaller than they are.) Porbeagle shark, which is commonly found in the north Atlantic (and is the one illustrated here), is said to make the best eating, while the mako shark, which lives in warmer waters, is popular in America.

Those who turn up their noses at the idea of eating shark may have been misled into believing that it has an unpleasant taste and is probably indigestible as well. A nineteenth-century writer on fish found in British waters stated that shark was used only for manure. And it is odd to find Larousse, in one dismissive sentence on shark, making a rare misjudgment, while being amusingly politically incorrect: 'The flesh of the shark, though very tough, is used as a foodstuff by the Lapps and by some negro peoples who are very partial to it.' This is nonsense. Not only is the flesh not tough, but it is also often enjoyed by the French who refer to it as *'veau de mer'*.

Such a comparison is explained by the pale colour of the flesh, by its tenderness and, because sharks are cartilaginous, the absence of bones. It is therefore most frequently sold, like tuna and swordfish, in steaks. The other day I dipped a few chunks of porbeagle shark in flour and egg, then coated them with a mixture of breadcrumbs, chopped anchovy fillets and parsley. After frying them in butter and oil and adding lemon juice, the result was judged to be very satisfactory, with a texture and flavour quite like swordfish or tuna – or even veal. Some books refer to the dryness of the shark's flesh and advise larding it with bacon fat.

I like the idea of the recipe provided by Alan Davidson, the distinguished author of seafood books, from his time as British ambassador in Laos. Garlic is fried with coriander leaves, puréed tomato and fresh lime juice, then poured over pieces of shark which are baked with a sprinkling of dried chilli pepper. For something hotter, Rick Stein recommends shark vindaloo, made with a fiery curry paste, fried onions and tomatoes and deseeded green chillies. A little water is added to the pan and the shark is simmered in the sauce for about 10 minutes.

Shark's fin soup I am happy to leave to the Chinese. Having seen a bowl recently in a Chinese restaurant, I decided to go for the razor clams and soft-shell crabs instead, which were not only more appealing but cheaper, too. I would also advise against shark pâté, or at least the tinned version from South Africa which I have been given. It tasted rather like a stale pilchard paste.

The shark does have relatives – tope, smooth hound, dogfish – which are frequently found in British waters. Dogfish usually appears at the fishmonger's as rock salmon, while the other two, because of their ammoniac smell, are sometimes ironically called sweet william. They are not bad when barbecued on a skewer with smoked bacon, peppers and mushrooms; if you read Jane Grigson on tope, you may think it worth cooking in a number of ways.

A year or more ago, I was bemused to notice that ITV was devoting most of one evening's viewing to the shark, with a documentary on killer sharks, yet another showing of *Jaws* and (appalling idea) something called *Celebrity Shark Bait*. It would have been more interesting to learn what happens to the huge number of sharks killed every year (about a hundred million worldwide), and to hear from those – in view of the statistics, presumably an increasing number – who enjoy eating them.

For those unfamiliar with shark, try a steak from whatever species is on sale or, if in Spain, look out for cazón, *which is the smooth hound and makes good eating.*

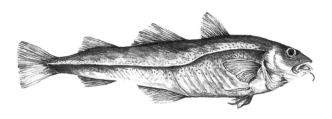

Cod

For the first time since childhood, I am taking cod liver oil again. Having visited Iceland (to fish for salmon) I was intrigued by the bottle of thick yellow liquid on the breakfast table, from which our Icelandic host and his wife took a dessert-spoonful every morning. Not only is it good for the joints and veins, but the Icelandic population, according to Daniel Hannan, writing in *The Spectator*, now has the longest life expectancy of any country in the world (I think Japan's is a bit longer). No doubt this has to do with the bracing climate and the outdoor life, but who is to say that a diet of cod and cod liver oil is not also a factor? For those, like me, who would rather not swallow fish oil in the morning with tea, toast and marmalade, the capsules will surely do the job just as well.

While cod is now said to be an endangered species in the North Sea, the Icelanders are managing their plentiful stocks very successfully. The cod wars of the 1970s may be a painful, if distant, memory, but one cannot really blame Iceland for imposing its 200-mile limit when the country's economy is so dependent on fish; and one can only look on enviously at its decision to stay out of the European Union, and thus keep foreign predators away from its waters. There are now so many cod off the north coast, one fisherman told me, that they have been eating young salmon in the fjords.

I hadn't realised that, apart from its huge exports of fresh cod, Iceland is also responsible for most of the salt cod which is sold in the EU. And, in addition to the cod's roe and liver, a commercial market has been found for cod's heads, dried over steam from hot thermal springs and sold to West Africa where they are valued as an aphrodisiac.

Without seeking to defend the overfishing of cod, both in the North Sea and in the Atlantic off Newfoundland, where European fishermen have been catching cod since the fifteenth century, it is now the case that, by being scarcer, cod is more socially acceptable. When, years ago, a friend of my father would say dismissively that 'cod is for servants', it accounted for half of all white fish landed at British ports and could therefore be judged common in both senses of the word. Escoffier was prescient in writing that if there were not such an abundance of cod, ' it would be held in as high esteem as salmon'. When perfectly fresh, I would suggest that it is held in higher esteem, and is rightly more expensive, than farmed salmon.

Many of us can remember being given overcooked cod in a watery sauce, prompting the comment – I don't know who said it first – about a piece of cod which passeth all understanding. But if the fish is fresh, preferably having been caught inshore on a long line, and correctly cooked, it can be judged with the best. I have not been to Aldeburgh lately, but I hope the fish huts are still there at the back of the shingle beach, from which you could buy codling line-caught the previous night from open boats.

Whether baked in a hot oven or grilled under a high heat, skin-side up, the fish should not need more than seven or eight minutes for the flesh to be white and moist, allowing the flaked pieces to fall away. Sauces for cod used to be made with butter, flour and milk, adding parsley or chopped hard-boiled egg; but I prefer something sharper such as a *sauce ravigote* or *rémoulade*, or a *beurre blanc*. Mashed potato made with olive oil, cream, garlic and saffron also goes very well. Delicious as it is, battered cod and chips is best left to those places which have deep fat fryers, although I have successfully fried cod cheeks in egg and breadcrumbs.

With salt cod, I confess, I am not very familiar. It has a stronger flavour, of course, than fresh cod, but since it is almost impossible to buy outside London, I may have to salt it myself (remembering to soak it in water for hours before cooking). In the 1930s, Madame Prunier listed 27 recipes for salt cod (*morue*), but it does not seem to be so popular these days, either in England or France – except for the *brandade de morue* (mashed salt cod and potato, with olive oil, garlic and cream) which is generally eaten in the south during Lent. I have made a passable *brandade* using smoked cod, eating it with a beetroot salad.

If you can buy cod caught from a small boat on a long line, it will be fresher than the deep-sea trawled stuff from Icelandic waters. For those unwilling to eat what they consider an endangered species, farmed cod was first marketed in 2006. Rick Stein explains how to salt cod in his book, English Seafood Cookery.

Skate

Skate or ray, either will do, although one thinks of the former name when the fish is eaten, and of rays as the larger and sometimes intimidating specimens, like the giant stingray I remember watching, and hearing, every evening at dusk in the British Virgin Islands, as it leapt out of the water just beyond the reef. There are big fellows, too, to be caught off the Hebrides, and a fisherman has recorded that the stomach of one monster contained two plaice, a lobster, several mackerel and a salmon.

But the skate wings that we buy are from creatures, usually the thornback ray or the common skate, tiny by comparison. If you should catch one yourself – skate spend much of their time lying on sandy areas of the seabed – don't make the mistake of eating it too soon, as the flesh will be tough. This is one of the very few fish that will benefit from keeping for two or three days; Welsh fishermen, I have read, will hammer a nail through the head of a skate and hang it on the door of a garden shed. But if it is left there for loo long, it will develop an unpleasant ammoniac smell.

This may have something to do with the fact that skate, like sharks, have skeletons of cartilage rather than bone. If your skinned wing is *à point*– it certainly won't be too fresh if bought in a supermarket, and the customers would soon complain if they sniffed ammonia at the fish counter – then it is worth cooking in the classic way, with black butter. The bible (aka Elizabeth David's *French Provincial Cooking*) decrees that the skate should be laid in a pan of cold water, with a sliced onion, parsley, salt and vinegar. Simmer for 15 minutes, then keep the fish warm while the butter is heated in a frying-pan. As soon as the butter begins to turn brown, pour it over the skate, together with a little wine vinegar, briefly boiled in the same pan with capers.

As Mrs David says: 'The ideal is only attained when the dish is set before those who are to eat it with the sauce absolutely sizzling.' I am not sure that I have ever experienced this ideal, which is why, when I eat skate two or three times a year, I am always slightly disappointed.

I doubt whether skate baked on a bed of vegetables and herbs, or with a cheese sauce, would be any more interesting. But I have enjoyed skate fried in batter with onion rings and fried parsley; and I have recently been playing with two recipes for skate eaten cold, which have turned out rather well.

Skate and its 'bones' are so naturally gelatinous that, having been poached in a *court bouillon* with white wine, the liquor will set when cold, making it ideal for a jellied terrine. This is made by combining the pieces of flaked fish with chopped shallot and parsley, then packing the mixture into a tin with the cold liquid. When refrigerated for several hours, the terrine can be sliced and eaten with a *sauce gribiche*, which is basically mayonnaise to which chopped egg, gherkins, capers, chervil and mustard have been added. This is delicate and delicious; for a more strongly flavoured and simpler first course, chef Fergus Henderson, of the award-winning London restaurant St John, recommends mixing the cold fish (poached in the same way and removed from the wings) with mashed anchovies and garlic, oil and red wine vinegar, plus a salad of chicory, rocket, parsley and capers.

Skate liver is said to be tasty – Larousse lists three recipes for it – but I have never found it in any fishmonger's. One recent discovery, however, was made last spring in the

Marlborough market, where a Suffolk fishmonger was selling skate knobs. These are apparently taken from the top of the wing, nearest the body, and look rather like cod cheeks. I have read nothing of them in any cookbook, but they are available at this time of year and are cheaper per pound than the wings. Coat the knobs in egg and breadcrumbs and fry them in oil; with lemon juice, a little tartare sauce and mashed potato, they make a very satisfying supper.

The thornback ray is generally thought to produce the best skate wings, although the fishmonger may not know from which species his skate comes. You could impress, or irritate, him by asking. Common skate is not so common any more.

Turbot / Brill

Y ou don't often see a large turbot these days. My guess is that the big ones, like most of the lobsters and crabs caught in our waters, go to Spain or France. The specimen which I saw in Paris last month was being cut into fat steaks for sale at €90 per kilo, or about £27.50 per pound. Perhaps there is no market in Britain for the king of white fish at this sort of price.

I have in the larder a long, oval fish kettle suitable for salmon, but I wonder whether or not anyone still uses the diamond-shaped kettle which was designed, probably in the nineteenth century, to take large flat fish, and especially turbot. In France it is called a *turbotière*, and is no doubt still in service in grand kitchens. A 25-pound turbot is not unusual; when cooked it can be simply lifted by the handles of the perforated rack which sits inside the kettle.

Brillat-Savarin was said to have been invited one evening to cook a large turbot in a country house which had no *turbotière*. He found instead a flat wine pannier of a suitable size to hold the fish and covered it with chopped onions and herbs. The turbot was then laid on top, covered with a washtub, and steamed over a water-boiler on top of the stove. The great epicure commented afterwards that the excellence of the dish caused him no surprise.

The fish which I was able to buy the other day weighed two pounds, cost a little less than £13 and was an ideal size for two people. (This was a wild fish, but farmed turbot of a similar size are often available.) I cut a slit down the middle of its back (dark skin), then poached it gently in water and milk with a few lemon slices. A sauce was made with butter, cream and mushrooms, adding – apparently from a Danish recipe – a little fresh grated horseradish, which seemed to lift the delicate flavour of the turbot.

Myrtle Allen, the original owner of Ballymaloe House in County Cork (the only public restaurant I know where you are offered a second helping), has a way with turbot which involves making an incision in the dark skin all around the fish, as close as possible to the fins – which some say are a great delicacy, although I cannot confirm this. Having baked the fish in a little water, she lifts the skin and pours over the white flesh a herb butter made with chopped thyme, chives and parsley. New potatoes are the only vegetable recommended. Although I think that turbot is best cooked on the bone, a piece from a large fish, bought if possible for a little less than £27.50 per pound, can be successfully grilled, although it should be basted with butter during the cooking. It goes well with a hollandaise sauce, or one made with shrimps and cream.

In the days of *turbotières*, the similar-looking, but smaller and more humble brill was considered a poor man's fish. Today, brill is a very acceptable substitute for the two- to three-pound 'chicken' turbot – so acceptable, in fact, that it is only a few pence cheaper per pound. But it does not have what Jane Grigson calls the 'tender firmness' of turbot. While not perhaps wishing to go as far as Madame Prunier – she invented a sort of brill and salmon sandwich, spread with salmon mousse – the combination of brill and shellfish can be rewarding. In Cornwall, where the brill are often line-caught, I have baked some skinned fillets in olive oil with shallots and various herbs, then mixed crab meat (white and brown), melted butter and capers, together with the shallots, herbs and pan juices. The capers were a particularly good addition to the dish, which we ate with braised fennel.

Continuing the theme, and consulting a few cookery
books, I find recipes for brill with mussels, with oysters
and with scallops. One might combine all three shellfish,
adding a sauce made with their liquor, cream, lemon juice,
tarragon and cayenne pepper. Another idea which appeals
to me is to bake a whole brill, or turbot, in a marinade of
anchovy sauce, olive oil, vinegar and paprika. It might go
rather well with a salad of sliced tomato, onion and mint
leaves, and might even have impressed the author of *The
Physiology of Taste*, Jean Anthelme Brillat-Savarin.

*To be sure of distinguishing between a turbot and
a brill, which are otherwise quite similar, the
turbot has little bony swellings on its back, while the
brill has scales.*

Anchovies

I'm not sure that I have ever seen a whole anchovy, freshly caught with its head on. They are to be found in Mediterranean markets, especially between Nice and Catalonia, and have a greenish-coloured back when fresh, which soon turns to grey-blue and then almost black. Anchovies can apparently be distinguished from sprats or small sardines by the size of the mouth, which stretches almost to the gills. Many times in Spain I have eaten fried anchovies, which are called *boquerones* in their fresh state, the name presumably referring to the fish's mouth – from *boca* (opening or mouth) and *boquear* (to gape). So it was a bit of a surprise to see in my Spanish cookbook that *boquerones* are translated as smelts – a fish that I had not heard of for some years.

Digressing slightly for a moment, smelts may be unknown to younger readers, because they do not seem to appear any more on fishmongers' slabs or restaurant menus. But I can certainly remember eating them years ago, in London and East Anglia, when they would have come from the Thames estuary. The smelt is classified as a freshwater fish because, despite living in the sea, it spawns a little way up river. According to Larousse, it smells of violets and its French name is *éperlan*, or pearly fish, for its pure whiteness. It certainly used to be commonly found in Normandy. *Où sont les éperlans d'antan?* I wonder if someone can enlighten me.

Anyway, I am pretty sure that the *boquerones* of Spain are not smelts, although both anchovies and smelts are deliciously delicate when fresh, rolled in flour and fried in oil. After removing the head and backbone, Spanish anchovies are also marinated in vinegar, then kept in olive oil, to be offered not only in every tapas bar in Spain, but also, nowadays, by almost every English fishmonger and supermarket. As a quick starter, with hunks of fresh bread and perhaps a little chopped garlic and parsley, they are hard to beat.

But it is, of course, the salted and skinned brown anchovy fillets that we know best. The salting of anchovies has its origins in antiquity: the process was certainly known to the

Greeks, and in Roman cookery the insides of the fish went into the making of a pungent sauce called *garum*. The popularity of anchovies in Europe was maintained for hundreds of years, largely because, moving around in shoals, they were easily caught in large numbers and stored in barrels of brine. Anchovy essence makes its appearance in late-eighteenth-century England, used not only with fish, but to sharpen up a meat stew (an early example of surf 'n turf?). Anchovy butter and anchovy sauce were becoming popular around this time, and then, in 1828, a certain John Osborn created and marketed a spiced anchovy mixture which has been known ever since as *patum peperium* or 'The Gentleman's Relish'. (Something else of lasting significance occurred in that seminal year, when a newspaper called *The Spectator* began weekly publication.)

I associate this paste, spread on hot, buttered toast, with Edwardian teas and dark winter afternoons and log fires, and hope it is still enjoyed in many houses today. The makers of 'The Gentleman's Relish' now also recommend that it be added to other food: onion soup, Welsh rarebit or scrambled eggs (a variation on Scotch woodcock). In Provence you will find the French equivalent, which is called *anchoïade*, and consists of pounded anchovy fillets and garlic, thinned with olive oil and vinegar. This paste is then spread on a thick slice of bread, toasted on the underside, and heated in the oven.

It is really quite remarkable how versatile this little fish can be. The Victorians were especially enthusiastic, prompting Mrs Beeton to give recipes for anchovy eggs, tartlets, biscuits, éclairs, fingers. There is a reference in *Great Expectations* by Charles Dickens to an anchovy sauce cruet. And in another old cookbook I have found anchovy stuffing (for waterfowl). One might argue, I suppose, that in English cooking salted anchovies belong to the past, but they remain essential today in popular dishes like *salade niçoise* and the warm sauce (*bagna cauda*) used as a dip for raw celery and peppers. When anchovies, in some guise – you can even buy anchovy purée in a tube – are eaten with eggs, cheese, vegetables, meat, one may occasionally forget that these little wonders have come from the sea.

Fresh anchovies are sometimes landed alongside sprats; some of the largest stocks are taken in the Bay of Biscay. Fishworks have them for sale, although not on a regular basis.

Bream / Bass

A bass, I have always thought, is a bass, but these days it is called sea bass – quite redundantly, since freshwater bass are not known in Europe. The bream of the sea, on the other hand should be distinguished from the freshwater fish of the same name which is related to carp. Instead, it is usually referred to only by its colour – black, red or gilthead; but if it is described simply as 'sea bream', which I have seen on an expensive London restaurant menu, then make sure you know which one you are getting.

In North America, sea bream is known as porgy, a name by which it was presumably also once called in south-west England, judging by this delightful old ballad:

> 'Me father was the keeper of the Eddystone Light,
>   And he slept with a mermaid one fine night;

From this union there came three –
A porpoise, and a porgy, and the other was me.'

Bream is an attractive, stocky little fish – it seldom
weighs much more than one pound – with a rather Roman
nose. The black variety, which is commonly caught off our
coasts, is said to be inferior in flavour to the other two,
although Cornishmen would dispute this. The red bream,
which has more of an orange-coloured skin and is not to
be confused with the inferior redfish (also known as
Norway haddock), has a wonderfully firm flesh, but it has
to be admitted that, on its own, baked or grilled, it does
not have the delicacy of flavour of its gilthead cousin. In
view of its texture, it is ideally suited for sashimi, skinned,
sliced and eaten raw with a soy sauce mixed with chopped
ginger, chives and fresh limes. I have read that the Japanese
are very partial to uncooked red bream, but this may be
a different fish from the European one.

There are, in fact, several varieties of bream to be found
in Mediterranean, and sometimes British, waters, of which
the gilthead is probably the best. Overall, it is silvery in
appearance; some heads are more gilt than others, but a
pale-coloured band should be visible between the eyes. It is
the sort of fish that one tends to remember by the place
where it was enjoyed on some past summer holiday – in
my case it was at a restaurant overlooking the harbour of

an island off the Croatian coast where the fish, caught that morning and grilled over charcoal, was as perfect as the surroundings. *Dorada a la sal* is a popular Spanish dish, where the whole fish is baked in a cake of salt, supposedly to ensure that the fillets do not dry up. This can also be achieved by baking the fish in foil, putting olive oil and perhaps a little mussel stock into the parcel.

In Spain you will also find bream called *besugo* and *urta*, but I'm not sure of the colour of their skins. They seem to benefit from the addition of garlic, green peppers and tomatoes in the cooking. The flavour may also be lifted by making slits along the flanks of the fish before sprinkling a mixture of, say, chopped parsley, thyme, shallots, capers and lemon slices over it and poaching it in white wine.

Bass is *bar* in France, or *loup de mer* (sea-wolf), presumably because it is a voracious eater of other fish. Like bream, it is often farmed these days. It may be my suspicious nature, but I often wonder when a fishmonger tells me that his bass are wild, whether and how he can be sure. The surest way is to catch your own in summer, when they come close inshore and into tidal estuaries and can be fished by casting from rocks or beach. When very fresh, bass and bream are best cooked whole (beware of the bass's viciously spiked dorsal fin) and cooked simply, and both seem to me to go perfectly with sliced fennel softened in butter and water.

If roasting bass in the oven, turn the heat up high and put some fennel and parsley (leaves and stalks) into the pan with lemon juice and olive oil. For those who insist on adding more flavours, it is worth trying ginger, spring onions and coriander leaves – although I would avoid the stronger flavours of chopped chilli and garlic. Pernod is sometimes used in a sauce or mayonnaise with such fish, but I think I shall stick with sorrel, or possibly saffron or – my great favourite among sauces for white fish – *beurre blanc*.

Both sea bream and sea bass are widely farmed and available all year round in uniform size. A large wild bass is worth waiting for; so is a wild gilthead bream, at its freshest in the Mediterranean.

Sturgeon

Many of us, not being regular purchasers of the sturgeon's eggs, will be unaware of the gravity of the caviar crisis. I have only just learnt that the population of the beluga sturgeon, which produces the best quality caviar and lives mostly in the Caspian Sea, has suffered a 90% decline in the past 20 years. It would seem that the fishing in this sea was much better regulated in the days of communism in the Soviet Union and the Shah's regime in Iran. But the independent, not to say irresponsible, Russians, Azerbaijanis, Kazakhs and Turkmen, and the Iranians, without any joint agreement to protect this hugely valuable resource, have so ruthlessly overfished the Caspian (often by poaching in each other's waters) that the beluga sturgeon has now been hunted almost to extinction.

Something like 70% of the exported beluga caviar goes to the United States. Its Natural Resources Defense Council (NRDC) has been trying for several years to get the fish listed as an endangered species, but it was only in 2005 that the import of beluga caviar into America from the Caspian and Black Seas was banned. If some cooperation between the littoral states can be achieved while demand is stifled, the beluga will surely return. Until then, deprived caviar consumers will have to make do with the other two species which secrete the delectable black roe – oscetra and sevruga.

The sturgeon, of which there are well over 20 different species, is a remarkable prehistoric fish which has been around since the time of the dinosaurs. The beluga sturgeon can weigh more than 2,000 pounds and live for 100 years. We certainly don't want to lose it. Some of the smaller varieties are seen in Atlantic waters (sturgeon go into fresh water to spawn), and in the nineteenth century they appeared quite commonly in England. It was Edward II who first proclaimed sturgeon to be a 'royal fish', but I doubt if it has appeared at a royal dining table in this country for some generations.

Mrs Beeton offers three recipes for sturgeon, but you are unlikely to find it on a fishmonger's slab these days, which is a pity since its firm, meaty appearance and taste are not unlike swordfish or shark. It is not as if all sturgeon are endangered, merely that they are no longer caught in British waters. Or, if they are, they are sold to France and Italy where there is a market for the fish, both wild and farmed. Madame Prunier, in her *Fish Cookery Book*, having commented that the flesh of the sturgeon 'needs a good deal of culinary skill to make it palatable', then proceeds to give four perfectly simple recipes. One involves nothing more than baking sturgeon steaks in white wine and fish stock, then making a *beurre blanc* from the cooking liquid. In Italy, the fish is often marinaded in olive oil, garlic and herbs before being grilled or fried. I have enjoyed smoked sturgeon, thinly sliced, but it is hard to find.

I had heard that sturgeon were occasionally caught in the mouth of the Guadalquivir river in south-west Spain, but there was no sign of them, or their eggs, when I was there recently, staying in the town of Sanlucar de Barrameda. We feasted instead on *puntillitas* (minuscule squid), *ortiguillas* (sea anemones) and *huevas de choco* (cuttlefish roe), milky-white and looking rather like little pearl earrings. This set me thinking about the other fish roes that are generally available these days.

None of them should strictly be called caviar, but the word now seems to embrace all roe of the same blackish colour – from lumpfish, capelin and herring (known as avruga). I find that lumpfish roe makes a good supper dish when spooned into a baked potato with sour cream, chopped shallot and a squeeze of lemon juice. Red lumpfish roe is also sold, but it's not as good as the salmon roe's larger eggs, which burst tastily in your mouth.

In America, white sturgeon are farmed; their caviar, described as comparable to Russian caviar, should help to fill the beluga gap, but I cannot vouch for its flavour.

For vegetarians, there is a product called Cavi-art, made from seaweed, which I think I can do without. More intriguing is the enterprise of a Yorkshireman who is planning to farm sturgeon, and market caviar, in Wakefield. His idea is to make a compost of shredded waste cardboard and horse-muck, feed it to worms and feed the worms to sturgeon in tanks which will grow up to be marketable fish producing lots of lovely caviar. Such a madcap scheme deserves to succeed.

If sturgeon is too difficult to obtain, and caviar too expensive, try some of the cheaper substitutes: the roe of lumpfish, herring, trout or flying fish.

Eel

We are in danger of losing our eels. To many people this may be of little interest, but it is a serious matter. The vast numbers of baby eels (elvers) which cross the Atlantic from the Sargasso Sea, somewhere near Bermuda, and end up in European rivers two or three years later have been falling dramatically. Many are being netted offshore, but the principal explanation blames the warming of the Arctic Ocean, resulting in weaker currents to carry the elvers to their destination. When they struggle into the river estuaries, and begin the last stage of their journey upstream, they may meet modern sluices without eel passes, or they may meet polluted water and die of disease. The eel catchers of the East Anglian fens (eels from Ely, geddit?) have been banned by the Environment Agency and an ancient way of life is coming to an end.

None of this makes any difference to the British market for eels, which today scarcely exists. Jellied eels we all know about, and they can still be bought; but where are the eel pies, the eel puddings and the eel soups of yesteryear? (Apart from Eel Pie Island at Twickenham, there is an intriguingly named pub, The Eel's Foot, out in the marshes of east Suffolk; its sign shows an eel peering from an old boot.)

Time was, in the nineteenth century, when cargoes of eels were sent from Holland to London, but now the trade is all the other way. Three-quarters of the eel catch in Lough Neagh, the largest eel fishery in the United Kingdom, now goes to Amsterdam, but numbers are severely reduced: elvers are being caught for European eel farms and, for whatever reason, too few are coming up the River Bann and into the lough.

Smoked eel is popular in this country and makes an excellent first course with horseradish sauce and brown bread and butter, but it is just as likely to have been smoked in Holland as in Britain. Can we not revive the fashion for fresh eel, which is appreciated in every other European country and which I have hugely enjoyed in recent weeks? I am ashamed to say that, at a family party of 10 in a Chinese restaurant in London, when I chose stewed eels in black bean sauce, only two others agreed to try even a small mouthful of this delicious dish. The eel was oily and rich, but also delicate in flavour. Don't take it from me, but read what that great fish cookery writer, Jane Grigson, has to say: 'I love eel. Sometimes I think it's my favourite fish.'

The problem is in finding your eel. Unless you have access to a Chinese fishmonger, or a coarse fisherman, or someone who buys eels for smoking, you may have to go to Billingsgate. The other day, a friend brought me back a live two-pounder from there. I had been warned that eels continue to wriggle after they are dead, but I was not expecting mine still to be slithering about on the dish several minutes after I had decapitated and gutted it. There are complicated ways of removing the skin, using string and pliers, but the easier method is to cut the eel into little steaks and let the skin fall off after cooking.

Following a recipe from south-west France, I fried shallots, mushrooms and bacon, then the eel briefly on both sides, and made a *roux* with the juices, flour and wine (both colours). Prunes, which had been soaked in wine overnight, were added to the dish, and everything was then gently stewed, with a *bouquet garni*, for an hour. The result was loudly acclaimed by the cook and several discerning guests. Eel-fanciers may also extol the virtues of the conger and the sharp-toothed Mediterranean moray, but I think they are best considered as material for soups. When I met Michel Roux the other day, he urged me to go and eat lampreys in Bordeaux, which may be a treat next year.

Elvers from the River Severn used to be available here in spring, but now they are transported to Europe and the Far East. You have to go to Spain to eat them, cooked in olive oil, garlic and red chilli and eaten with a wooden fork, but these *angulas* cost about £20 for a fairly modest portion. The good news is that the enterprising Spanish now make what are called *gulas*, from white fish *transformado* to look and taste like the real thing. They are one-tenth of the price and not bad at all.

In parts of Italy, close to the Adriatic coast, roast eel will be served, as it always is, on Christmas Eve. If I can find an eel in time, we shall follow that tradition in Cornwall this year, then have a little smoked eel the next day before the turkey.

I have since come across an even better recipe for fresh eel. Having fried the eel fillets or pieces, make a sauce with sorrel, spinach, parsley, tarragon, wine, butter and cream and pour this over the fish on croutons of fried bread.

Scallops

Lunching at the Fishworks restaurant in Bath, I was intrigued to see Isle of Skye diver-caught scallops on the menu. Would divers from Skye, however hardy or intrepid, be plunging into those stormy, if not icy, Hebridean waters in winter? Surely the scallops had been dredged, or possibly frozen since the summer? No, the waiter assured me, they were caught by a husband and wife working together, who always dived for scallops at this time of year. Whether the scallops taste better if lifted from the seabed by hand rather than by net, I rather doubt, but one can have nothing but admiration for these Skye divers prepared to suffer for our enjoyment.

The scallop is one of the very few bivalves capable of swimming, by opening and clapping its two shells together, rather in the manner of cymbals. Its fan-shaped shell may be familiar to many from the logo adopted years ago by the Shell oil company, but it has a rather more interesting and ancient history. James, son of Zebedee, and one of the inner circle of apostles, was unreliably reported to have gone to Iberia to preach the gospel after his master had ascended into heaven. Having been slain by the Jews, James's remains were being carried by ship from Palestine to Spain when, off the coast of Portugal, his followers rescued from the sea a man and his horse covered with scallop shells. Thus did the shell become the emblem of St James, carried by pilgrims to his shrine at Santiago de Compostela; and hence *coquilles St Jacques*.

Many of us remember the rather heavy dish of scallops Mornay which used to be the only way they were offered in restaurants. The shellfish were cooked in a white sauce with grated cheese and served in the shell with mashed potato decoratively piped round the rim. One then took the shell home and used it as an ashtray. I think I began to appreciate scallops about 30 years ago in Biarritz, when I came across them sautéed in butter and parsley with a splash or two of whisky. Today their popularity in Britain, and their price, seem to be going up all the time.

Oddly enough, I have only ever found scallops in one part of Spain, in St James's Galicia. As a mainly Atlantic shellfish, they don't play a great role in Italian cooking. But they are much enjoyed on the other side of the ocean, in the United States, although it comes as no surprise to learn that Americans discard the delicious orange coral – which is a bit like their absurd, cholesterol-fanatical insistence on eating an omelette made with only the white of the egg.

Frozen scallops are best avoided: they may have been soaked in water to enlarge them before freezing, they lose flavour when thawed, and they will go back to their original size when cooked. The freshest ones are almost translucent and have a sweetness and tenderness which make them suitable to be sliced and eaten raw, dipped in a mixture of soy sauce, grated ginger and fresh lime juice. Or the scallops might be marinated for an hour or so in fresh citrus juice (lemon and orange), together with olive oil, strips of red chilli and fennel leaves.

The cooking of scallops should be brief, either on a griddle or in a hot ridged pan to achieve those fashionable brown stripes; treated in this way, with pea purée and a mint vinaigrette, they have featured on the menu at the Kensington Place restaurant in London for the past 10 years or more. I have made a not unsuccessful stab at this excellent dish at home, stewing frozen peas with lettuce, spring onions, sugar and cream before putting them in a blender. A sharp vinaigrette made with chopped mint should be dripped over the griddled scallops. Jennifer Paterson (one of the televised *Two Fat Ladies*, who died in 1999) used to cook her scallops with shallots, vermouth and white wine, on a bed of stewed leeks, with a sauce consisting of cream and parsley added to the reduced leek, wine and scallop liquor.

Then there are those delectable little queen scallops which usually come from north Britain and especially around the Orkneys. Sautéed in butter with breadcrumbs, or with lemon juice, garlic and parsley, they make a good Sunday night supper, on salad leaves or toast. These days, the 'great' scallops (often incorrectly called 'king') are sometimes combined with a stronger flavour – bacon or smoked sausage. As a suggestion for Christmas, the scallops might be sandwiched between grilled foie gras and black pudding – before the fresh fish famine which, in Wiltshire at least, will last well into the new year while fishmongers and fish market stalls remain closed.

Here we shall have to survive on home-grown beef from our heifer, killed in October, and a barley-fed, hand-plucked, well-hung turkey from my son's farm in south Cornwall.

Be sure to buy fresh, not frozen, scallops, ideally in the shell and with their delicious coral or roe attached. Even if you prefer to cook scallops without the coral, it should be reserved for making a sauce at a later date.

Poultry and Game Suppliers

PETER FISHER GAME
175 Aylsham Road, Norwich, Norfolk NR3 2AD
01603 407415

BUTCHER & EDMONDS
6 Central Markets, Smithfield Market, London EC1A 9LH
020 7329 7388

EVERLEIGH FARM SHOP
Everleigh, Marlborough, Wiltshire SN8 3EY
01264 850344

Fish Suppliers

MARTIN'S SEAFRESH
St Columb Business Centre, Barn Lane, St Columb,
Cornwall TR9 6BU
01637 889168
www.martins-seafresh.co.uk

FISHWORKS
17 Belmont, Bath BA1 5DZ
0800 052 3717
www.fishworks.co.uk

STEVE HATT
88-90 Essex Road, London N1 8LU
020 7226 3963

Index of dishes